INDIAN PUBLIC WORKS

INDIAN PUBLIC WORKS

AND COGNATE INDIAN TOPICS

WILLIAM THOMAS THORNTON

GYAN

Published by

Gyan Publishing House
5, Ansari Road
Daryaganj, New Delhi-110002
Phone: 011-47034999, 9811692060
E-mail: books@gyanbooks.com

Distribution Network
gyanbooks.com
India, USA, Canada, UK, Australia

ISBN: 978-93-7225-099-2 (PB)

First Published, 1875

2nd Impression 2025

Printed at: Gyan Press, Delhi.

INDIAN PUBLIC WORKS AND COGNATE INDIAN TOPICS
Author: WILLIAM THOMAS THORNTON

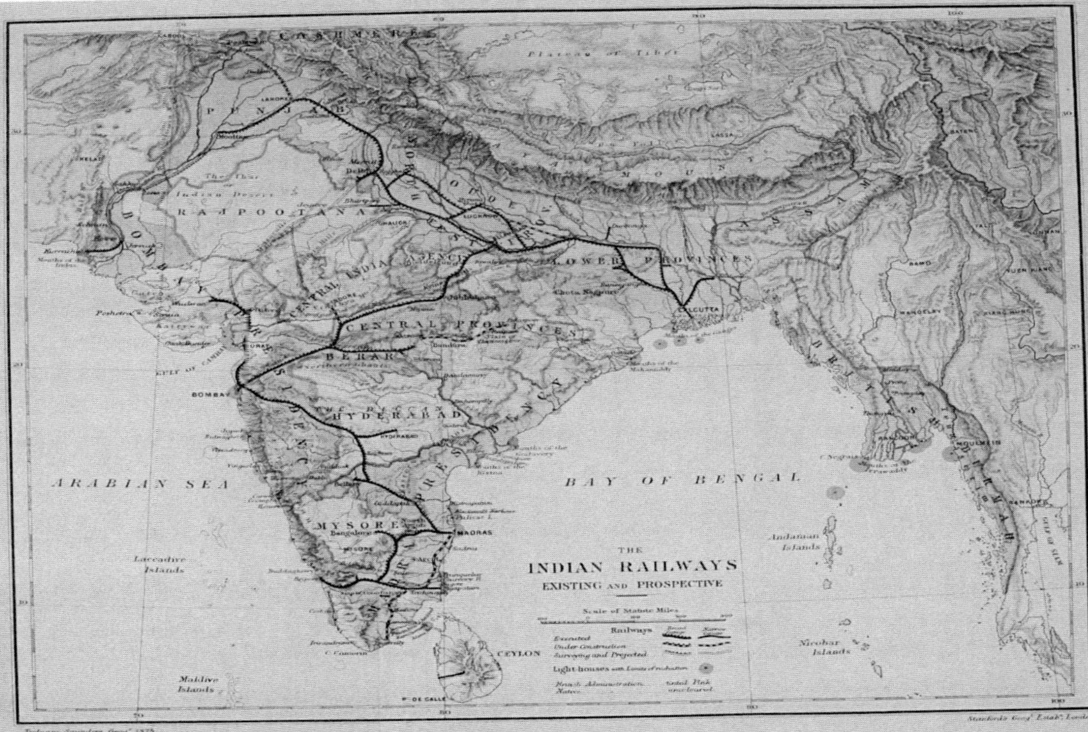

London Macmillan & C[o]

INDIAN PUBLIC WORKS

AND COGNATE INDIAN TOPICS

BY

WILLIAM THOMAS THORNTON, C.B.

SECRETARY FOR PUBLIC WORKS IN THE INDIA OFFICE
AUTHOR OF A TREATISE 'ON LABOUR' ETC.

1875

TO

GEORGE DOUGLAS

DUKE OF ARGYLL, K.T.

FOR FIVE YEARS

HER MAJESTY'S PRINCIPAL SECRETARY OF STATE FOR INDIA

THESE PAGES

TREATING FOR THE MOST PART OF

SUBJECTS WHICH THE AUTHOR HAS BEEN PRIVILEGED

TO DISCUSS WITH HIS GRACE

ARE INSCRIBED

WITH FEELINGS OF PERSONAL ATTACHMENT

NOT ALWAYS DEVELOPED OUT OF OFFICIAL SUBORDINATION

CONTENTS.

CHAPTER I.

INTRODUCTORY.

CHAPTER II.

COMMUNICATIONS.

CHAPTER III.

IRRIGATION.

CHAPTER IV.

MISCELLANEOUS WORKS.

CHAPTER V.

ESTABLISHMENTS.

CHAPTER VI.

LAND TENURE.

CHAPTER VII.

NATIONAL EDUCATION.

INDIAN PUBLIC WORKS.

CHAPTER I.

INTRODUCTORY.

PUBLIC WORKS have always formed rather a weak side of Anglo-Indian administration, and nothing can be farther from the design of this volume than to eulogize either the East India Company's management of them, or that of the Viceroyalty, by which the Company's domination has been superseded. It is, however, rather absolutely than relatively that the management of either has been at fault. Since the fall of the Roman Empire, there has never been a Government whose strong side has been Public Works; and among existing Governments, there certainly is not one which, from the height of these latter, would be warranted in casting disdainful glances on the Anglo-Indian. In those countries which are at present best provided with Public Works the provision has been made mainly by private enterprise, with little aid from the State, while in none of those countries in which the State has done most in this direction has it done nearly as much within an equal period as the British rulers of

India have done within the last twenty years. Since the Indian Public Works Department was constituted in 1855, its own proper expenditure, irrespectively of an about equal amount absorbed by guaranteed railways, has been more than ninety millions sterling, a very liberal tithe of the entire revenues of the State during the period, nor need the results of this enormous outlay shrink from comparison as to quality any more than as to quantity with those of corresponding governmental expenditure nearer home. Not to speak of the extension to Peshawur of the Indian Via Appia, the Grand Trunk Road already running for twelve hundred miles from Calcutta to Lahore, the Simla, Nynee Tahl, Raneekhet and Darjeeling Roads, scaling as they do the steeps and overhanging the abysses of the Lower Himalayas, would, each of them, be no mean match for the most remarkable of the Highland tracks commemorated in the immortal distich

> If you'd seen these roads before they were made,
> You'd have held up your hands, and blessed General Wade.

Nor would the glories of the Ganges, or Baree Doab, or Godavery, or Kistnah Canals pale beside those of the Caledonian. If, despite the long list of constructional successes of which these are samples, public works are still conspicuous in India far more by their absence than their presence, the reason is not so much that the Anglo-Indian Government has done little towards establishing them, as that preceding Governments, by doing next to nothing, left such an immensity for it to do.

In justification of this remark it may be proper here

to interpose a definition. By Public Works are, throughout the following pages, to be understood all such and only such fabrics or excavations as are designed rather for public than for private accommodation, for the use, that is, not of particular individuals but of any of the whole mass of individuals composing the nation who may be in a position to take advantage of them. Monuments of personal ostentation or magnificence, however grand in scale or artistic in design and execution, are excluded from the category. Imperial or Royal palaces or mausolea stand outside the line that marks as a class apart roads, railways, bridges, canals of irrigation or navigation, embankments, harbours, docks, lighthouses, law courts, barracks, and a variety of other edifices subservient to purposes of general administration, civil or military. Now although, according to Mountstuart Elphinstone, 'from the earliest Hindoo times to the decline of the Mogul Empire, the great roads were objects of much attention to the Government,' and although, according to the same historian, Ibn Batuta, travelling in the fourteenth century along the coast of Malabar, found the highways shaded by trees, with resting-houses and wells at regular intervals, it is not to be supposed that any of these highways were paved, while it is needless to insist on the instability of all unpaved roads of a pre-macadamite age. Although, too, in a list of works attributed to the Mogul Sovereign, Firooz Toghluk, one hundred and fifty bridges are included, it is not the less certain that, long after the latest Mogul dynasty had ceased to be more than the shadow of a great name, all the larger Indian rivers were still unbridged, that, until the present century was far advanced, none but a first-rate swimmer could cross the Jumna or Soane or Godavery or Kistnah, except by fording or ferrying, or can even now traverse the main stream of the Indus or Brahmaputra, or more than three or four of their affluents or branches, by any other means.[1] Although, again, irrigation received a good deal of attention long before aids to transport and locomotion began to be much thought of, that attention was bestowed rather by individual or associated landholders than by the State. Firooz Toghluk, over and above his one hundred and fifty bridges, is recorded to have constructed, for irrigational purposes, fifty dams across rivers, and thirty reservoirs, but the very number of these shows that they must have been in general of moderate size; while, with regard to the one irrigational canal with which the same monarch is credited, and which was designed to convey the waters of the Chetang to his hunting seat at Hissar, we are distinctly informed that, sixty years after his death, it had ceased to perform its office, a great part of its bed having become so filled up as to be scarcely discernible. Among other canals of some little antiquity, those of most historic celebrity are the two east and west of the Jumna, excavated at Shahjehan's behest by Alimurdan Khan, and of these the first became practically extinct about the middle of the eighteenth century, and the second seems to have been supplied with water for only one single season, if indeed for so long : when first sub-

[1] Over the Ganges there is now one solitary bridge, that of the Oude and Rohilcund Railway, at Rajghat, finished about a twelvemonth ago.

jected to the critical scrutiny of British engineers, neither the one nor the other had revolved any but sandy waves within the memory of the oldest inhabitant of the neighbourhood. It need scarcely be said that for navigation, whether internal or maritime, absolutely nothing was done by any Hindoo or Mahometan dynasty; that, under the sway of each, rivers and tides were left at their own caprice alternately to scoop out harbours and to silt them up; that not a lighthouse, still less a dock or breakwater, scarcely even a wharf or jetty, was to be seen along the whole Indian coast line. Of miscellaneous public edifices, colleges, hospitals, hill-forts, mosques, pagodas, there was no doubt comparative abundance, but few if any of these were at once suitable and available for the purposes of administration according to European notions. Briefly, then, the programme of constructional operations which the English in India found awaiting them as soon as they had time to look around them after becoming masters there, was of unprecedented length, so that, within the period that has since elapsed, the utmost energy on their part must have failed to discharge all its obligations. At least as much of praise is due for what they have done towards clearing off the score as of blame for what they have omitted, and if in the course of this volume more stress is nevertheless laid on their shortcomings than on their performances, the reason simply is that the most trustworthy guidance for the future is that which may be derived from the errors of the past.

According to Adam Smith, the moral obligations of a Government to its subjects are three in number :—Defence against foreign aggression and intestine commotion; protection from domestic injustice; erection and maintenance of public works and institutions, and the enumeration does not seem to be open to any serious exception. Still, however plainly incumbent it may be on a Government to see that all necessary public works are provided, much doubt may reasonably be entertained whether their actual provision is a function which any Government can be specially qualified to discharge. Smith, during his two years' residence in France as tutor to the young Duke of Buccleuch, had noticed more than one 'magnificent high-road made through a desert country where there was little or no commerce, merely because it happened to lead to the country villa of the intendant of the province or to that of some great lord to whom the intendant found it convenient to pay his court.' He had seen 'great bridges thrown over rivers at places where nobody passed, or merely to embellish the view from a neighbouring palace.' He had noticed too that although 'the great post roads—the roads which made the communication between the principal towns of the kingdom—were in general kept in good order, and in some provinces were even superior to the greater part of the turnpike roads in England; what we call the cross roads, that is, the far greater part of the roads of the country, were entirely neglected, and in many places absolutely impassable for any heavy carriage;' nay that 'in some places it was even dangerous to travel on horseback, and mules were the only conveyance which could safely be trusted.' 'The proud minister of an ostentatious ccurt may,' he says, 'frequently take pleasure in executing a work of splendour and magnificence such as a great highway which is frequently seen by the principal nobility whose applauses not only flatter his vanity, but even contribute to support his interest at court. But to execute a great number of little works, in which nothing that can be done can make any great appearance or excite the smallest degree of admiration in any traveller, and which, in short, have nothing to recommend them except their extreme utility, is a business which appears in every respect too mean and paltry to merit the attention of so great a magistrate.'[1] Nor is it only when personal motives interpose that the central authority or its representatives are likely to acquit themselves but indifferently in the capacity of constructors. Even when desirous of supplying what is requisite, they often, instead of consulting the party chiefly concerned, prefer to trust to their own skill in divination, and not unfrequently make in consequence somewhat erroneous guesses. For the expenses, too, of their constructional operations they can draw upon coffers which are replenished at expense of the sweat of other brows than theirs, and they are consequently relieved from one of the most cogent motives for avoiding waste. With respect to public works, the public may be presumed to know best both what the public wants and also how much the public can afford to pay in order to get its wants supplied; and the next best judges on these points would seem to be those private individuals who are ready to undertake the works as commercial speculations, and who, in order to make their

[1] 'Wealth of Nations,' Book v. ch. i. part iii.

venture a secure one, will do their best to avoid all works but those for the use of which the public may be expected to be willing to pay freely, doing their best also to make the money they lay out go as far as possible. For this reason there has always been a strong feeling in this country in favour of leaving public works to private enterprise, which moreover, may really deserve to be preferred wherever or as long as the only choice lies between it and the agency of an irresponsible Government. But in these days most civilized Governments are constantly becoming more and more responsible to public opinion, whose keen and even captious vigilance, when exerted through the medium of popular assemblies and an unfettered press, operates almost as effectually as feelings of self-interest could do to keep in check official vagaries, to restrain official extravagance, and to convert official apathy into activity. Witness on this head the exemplary efficiency of the British Post Office under the management, first of Sir Rowland Hill, and subsequently of those on whom Sir Rowland's mantle has fallen. Testifying, on the other hand, to the proneness of private enterprise, when once it has acquired the monopoly of any industrial field, to assume, together with the powers, all the airs of despotism, are certain appeals of our own to King Log for deliverance from King Stork, petitions to Parliament for purchase of railways by the State, vociferous denunciations at vestry meetings of the iniquities of gas and water companies. Perhaps it may here be suggested that what is thus sought is merely the lesser of two great evils, and we may be reminded of one stock objection to governmental interposition wherever it can be dispensed with. That the State should do nothing for the public which the public can do equally well for itself has almost passed into a proverb, the soundness of which I am myself so far from disputing that I should rather be disposed to carry the maxim to an extreme. To me the fostering of habits of self-help and self-dependence appears so important an element in national education that, within certain, and those pretty wide limits, I would say, Better for the public to do things badly for itself than to have them well done by private individuals. Evidently, however, what is done for the public by individuals the public does not do for itself, nor is there any way by which a public can exercise any executive functions except by delegating their execution to some presiding authority. Now publics are of various degrees and magnitudes—parochial, urban, metropolitan, provincial, national; but that must be a very small public indeed the members of which are not much too numerous to be capable of combining for constructional operations. Directly to participate in these, a parish must needs accept the agency of its vestry, a town of its municipality, a nation of its central government. Where, then, works of national dimensions are concerned, to say that the State should leave the public to construct them is a contradiction in terms, for in no other mode can the public undertake the construction than by entrusting it to the State.

Besides, it is plainly desirable, not simply that public works should be as suitable as possible for their special purposes, but also that the public should have the use of them on the lowest possible terms, which it obviously cannot have if private speculators are permitted to make a profit from them, while without the prospect of profit private speculators will not undertake them. That surely cannot be the best arrangement for the public under which public needs become the subject of private gain—under which particular persons profit at the expense of the generality. Evidently it were better either that the charges for use of public works should be so low as barely to cover expenses without yielding any surplus, or that, if any profits are made at the public expense, they should return into the public treasury. What private management of public works may become, at its worst, we may judge from what we are suffering from railway arrogance and recklessness ; but we may also perceive that at its best it must necessarily be far more costly than State management, properly controlled by public opinion, would be permitted to become. There is, too, a palpable fallacy at the bottom of the popular prepossession in favour of leaving public works to private enterprise. Private speculators, in spite of the warnings of self-interest, are liable to occasional miscalculation. They sometimes over-estimate public needs, or under-estimate the cost of providing for them, and so engage in undertakings for the use of which, when completed, the public cannot be induced to pay sufficiently to compensate the undertakers for their outlay. But any loss sustained by the undertakers, in consequence, is commonly regarded as exclusively theirs, and as being moreover partially counterbalanced by gain accruing to the public. A railway may be made through a district, the traffic of which is not sufficient to render the railway remunerative, but although in that case to have constructed the line at the public expense might at first sight seem necessarily a bad investment of public money, still to have the convenience of the railway is undoubtedly an advantage to the public, and it is not usually perceived to be any drawback from this advantage that to provide the convenience has cost certain private individuals more than it is worth, for no part of the cost is supposed to devolve on the public except what the public voluntarily pays in the form of rates and fares. With the private wealth sunk in the undertaking, the public is assumed to have no concern. It is curiously overlooked that the total of public wealth is but the sum of the portions of wealth possessed by the several private individuals composing the public, and that consequently no individual can misapply his own substance without simultaneously misapplying a portion of the national substance. Yet the loss resulting to the nation at large from such misapplication is manifestly as great as that which is sustained by the immediate owners of the misapplied wealth; nay, on examination it will be found to be even greater. If, for instance, in a country in which the current rate of profit is 10 per cent. per annum, a railway or other public work constructed by private enterprise, at the cost of a million sterling, and constructed, let us for convenience sake suppose, in the course of a single twelvemonth, cannot by the most skilful management be made to yield a net annual return of more than 3,000*l.*, or 3 per cent. on its cost, the shareholders obviously obtain 7,000*l.* a year less than they might have done by a different investment of their money. But it is not they alone who thus suffer. For, to say that the same million sterling, if employed in agricultural or manufacturing industry, might have yielded 10 instead of 3 per cent. is equivalent to saying that 100,000*l.* worth of goods might in that case have been added to the quantity sent to market, and thereby rendered available for distribution amongst, and consumption by, the entire community, which therefore has virtually sacrificed 100,000*l.* for the sake of convenience worth only 30,000*l.* Thus, equally with the shareholders, the entire community has lost 70,000*l.*, the effects of the loss making themselves felt nationally in the form of higher general prices. But this is not all. The million sterling which has been irrecoverably sunk in the supposed public work would, if invested as productively as it might have been, while bringing into existence 100,000*l.* of profit, have likewise reproduced itself. The necessaries of life, raw materials, &c., represented by the million sterling, would, after having been consumed or worked up, have been replaced by products capable of being exchanged for another million's worth of necessaries and materials, which in their turn might be consumed and worked up, similarly reproducing their own equivalent with 10 per cent. profit in addition, and the same process might be any number of times repeated. The million in question may be likened to the cruse of oil that failed not, and to the barrel of meal that wasted not, wherewith the widow of Sarepta went on making cakes without end. The nation, similarly, after eating its cake, might still have its cake, and by judicious perseverance in cake-making might go on for ever eating and still having. Now if, on the other hand, part of the national capital were withdrawn from such perennially fruitful confection, and expended on a comparatively sterile public work, the nation as a whole would not merely lose the profit that would otherwise have been annually made on the principal so withdrawn, but would be deprived also of the annual use of the principal itself, whereas the loss of the private owners of the principal would arise chiefly from the fact of their capital being hopelessly locked up in the public work, and would consist chiefly in the difference between the petty profits which the imprisoned capital was actually making, and the larger profit which it might have made if set free. Thus instead of the nation as a whole being unaffected by the disastrous speculations of private enterprise, its aggregate loss may far exceed that of the private undertakers immediately concerned, although the immense number of persons amongst whom the national loss is distributed, may prevent any one of them from being sensible of his share.

It is not indeed impossible for a country to be too rich to be affected in this manner. From our own country, literally overflowing as it is with wealth, with wealth increasing annually so fast that the whole annual increment cannot be employed at home at a rate sufficient to satisfy its owners, capital is habitually sent abroad for investment, the British public as a whole deriving subsequently little or no benefit from the portion so sent. For the British public, therefore, it may be better that its superabundant capital should be employed in any domestic undertaking whatever, not absolutely useless, than that it should be virtually lost to the nation by being invested, however profitably, in foreign countries; better certainly that it should be applied to the construction of London, Chatham, and Dover Railways, or of Southampton Docks, than be invested abroad even in the mines of St. John del Rey. But it is only in respect to an exceedingly wealthy country that the doctrine of the intimate connexion between personal and natural wealth requires to be thus qualified. In a country as poor as India, whose aggregate wealth is much below the amount that might forthwith find profitable occupation at home, it cannot but be nationally inexpedient that any public works should be constructed by private enterprise which it would not have been worth the public's while to construct at the public expense.

Out of these considerations arises another, more practically important, of a converse character. Public works, in which private enterprise could not engage without loss, may sometimes nevertheless be advisably undertaken at the public expense. A public work cannot adequately remunerate private undertakers unless the payments made by its immediate customers for its use are such as to yield adequate profit on its cost, but the same work may quite possibly be indirectly productive of compensating public advantages for which its immediate customers will not consent to pay. How this can be may not be readily apparent to us, seeing as we do that whatever be the benefits derivable from a public work, the first recipients of those benefits can be no other than those who make use of the public work, and that through their medium alone the benefits can be communicated to the general public. The truth of the statement may, however, be shown by examples, and by reference more especially to bridges, roads, railways, canals, and other aids to locomotion and transport. One chief use of these consists in diminishing the expense of access to old markets, and in rendering new markets accessible, thereby temporarily enabling producers to obtain augmented profits on their sales, and permanently encouraging them to extend production. It is the second of these operations which chiefly demands attention here.

If by means of a bridge thrown over a deep or rapid stream, goods can be carried to market more expeditiously or conveniently than was possible when boats or lighters were indispensable for the purpose, and if for the use of the bridge the very highest tolls be charged, that will not render that mode of conveyance more expensive than the previous one, and, nevertheless, the net revenue resulting be not sufficient to give the bridge-owners the average rate of profit on their outlay, the benefits afforded by the bridge will plainly have been produced at a cost exceeding their value; but, if so, not only must the construction of the bridge have been a bad investment on the part of its constructors, it would equally have been a bad investment if constructed at the public expense. Such highest tolls, however, are never really leviable. Ordinary people greatly dislike laying aside old habits, and require to be rather heavily bribed in order to be induced to adopt novel practices. A new bridge may offer a much quicker and easier means of getting themselves and their merchandise across a river, but if, for the time and trouble thereby saveable, they are to be charged as much or nearly as much as the saving is worth, they will see that they would gain little or nothing by changing, and will prefer adhering to the old familiar ways. In order, therefore, to get the bridge frequented, its owners have no alternative but to charge for its use considerably less than its use is worth, and the consequence is that the producers who avail themselves of it, and who, though by its aid conveying their goods to market somewhat more cheaply than before, are yet for awhile able to sell them as dearly as before, reap an extra profit which stimulates them to extend production. Farmers thereupon take fresh land into cultivation, or apply improved modes of culture to old land; manufacturers manufacture more largely, and an increased quantity of goods of all sorts is in consequence sent to market, and by lowering prices brings down profits eventually to the previous level. The traffic over the bridge, meanwhile, of course increases proportionably, but if nevertheless still insufficient to compensate the shareholders, it is not in the power of the latter to increase their revenue by levying enhanced rates. For with the rates as they actually are, producers are receiving only the old rate of profit, rather than submit to a reduction of which they would withdraw part of their capital from their business, thereby diminishing the traffic over the bridge. Yet though in this case the bridge would still be comparatively unprofitable, though it would remain an undertaking on which it was unwise for private enterprise to have engaged, it might now have become one on which public money might have been very profitably invested. For the enlargement of certain departments of productive industry, to which it had led, had necessarily involved the employment of additional capital in those departments, and, unless the country were very poor, this additional capital need not have been withdrawn from other businesses, but might consist of capital which, in the ordinary course of things, would have remained idle for a while, instead of being forthwith utilised. Whatever be the productive capacities of any place or district, its actual productiveness will be limited by the demand for its produce in the markets to which it has access, for, of course, neither agriculturists nor manufacturers will intentionally produce more than they expect to be able to dispose of. Most likely they may possess or might procure on credit additional capital to invest in their several businesses. There is always in store plenty of spare food and other necessaries suitable for the remuneration of labour, plenty of spare raw material to be worked up, plenty of spare tools and machinery to assist in the working; but agriculturists and manufacturers may have no inducement to extend the scale of their operations, and therefore all this spare capital is left in store till it is wanted. But now, if fresh markets be opened, this capital, instead of being left idle for a while, will be forthwith applied to production, and it is to be particularly noted that the increase of national wealth thereupon consequent will not be limited to the additional profits made by the local producers; will not consist of merely the 10 per cent. or other percentage gained by them on their increased investments; in other words, will not be simply the difference between cost of production and the market value of the goods produced, but will be more nearly the whole of that market value. Suppose that a farmer, who, while his market was comparatively limited, had, by expending the equivalent of 100 quarters of wheat in wages, seed, manure, &c. been accustomed to raise an average crop of 150 quarters, should, now that his market is enlarged, employ 200 quarters in producing 300 quarters, the addition made to the national wealth will not be 50 quarters merely, but 150 quarters. For the supplementary investment of 100 quarters, if not so employed, might have been left in the stacks for a year or more, being during the interval of no more use to the consuming public than if it had not existed, whereas, in the circumstances supposed, the 100 quarters have been consumed during the year, and yet at the end of it the public are in possession of 150 quarters in their place. The same thing, only in a less degree, would take place in regard to manufactures. So much of any additional investment in these as consisted of wages to operatives would have to be added to the manufacturer's net profit in order to show to what extent that investment had augmented national wealth.

It is thus clear that a bridge built at the public expense

may, by promoting the earlier utilisation of capital, easily occasion an addition to national wealth, amply sufficient to compensate for deficiencies in the net revenue resulting from tolls. And a similar inference might even more obviously be drawn if a railway instead of a bridge were selected by way of illustration. Since George Stephenson, in 1826, cut the first sod for the Manchester and Liverpool line, the expenditure on railways in the United Kingdom has altogether been upwards of 590 millions, or on an average more than twelve millions annually; but although the average rate of profit in this country on capital invested in productive industry would probably be greatly understated at 10 per cent., the net profits of British railway shareholders have not averaged more than 3½ per cent., so that their total net receipts in 48 years may be roughly reckoned at 494 millions. It may be true that the aforesaid 590 millions could not have found employment at home at the current rate of profit, but they could undoubtedly have earned at least that rate if judiciously invested abroad, in that case producing a net revenue of nearly 1,412 millions altogether, so that by preferring to spend it on railways at home the shareholders have incurred a loss of 918 millions. But, on the other hand, the exports from and the imports into the United Kingdom, which in 1826 were 56,000,000*l.* and 44,000,000*l.*, were in 1873, 311,000,000*l.* and 371,000,000*l.* respectively—having increased during the interval at an average rate of about 5 and 7 millions annually. The increase of exports and imports is of course a very imperfect measure of the contemporaneous increase of nationa wealth, but, even as thus imperfectly indicated, the addition made since 1826 cannot be less than 8,000 millions; and although free trade and a variety of other causes have no doubt contributed immensely to this result, still the portion of it remaining due to railways is, as indubitably, also immense—quite immense enough, if distributed rateably amongst railway shareholders, to bring up their average dividends from 3½ to 10 per cent. But, if so, it follows that the same enormous network of railways which to private enterprise has proved a losing concern, would, if constructed at the public expense, have turned out to be a very lucrative investment of public money. Wherefore, if private enterprise had not interposed, it would have been highly expedient for the public to construct all the railways at its own cost. True, overflowing as the United Kingdom does with capital which cannot find adequately remunerative occupation at home, it is still better for the nation as a whole that some of its individual members have relieved it from the necessity of making railways at the public cost, by making them with money which would otherwise have been lost to the nation as a whole by being sent abroad; but it is only when a country is literally overflowing with wealth that this can be the case. In a country whose entire capital is ordinarily retained at home for immediate or early employment in productive industry, it is quite possible for public works, constructed at the public expense with money raised by general taxation, to be unremunerative directly, and yet indirectly to repay the public well, although, if the same works had been constructed by private speculators, there might be nothing, unless perhaps the sense of having made private sacrifice for the public good, to compensate the individual speculators for the losses sustained by them.

The comparison thus attempted between the advantages and disadvantages of governmental agency and of private enterprise, abstractedly considered, will not, it is hoped, be deemed misplaced, notwithstanding that the question, in its abstract form, may probably never have presented itself to the Anglo-Indian Government, which has never really been allowed a choice between the rival agencies. In India, not only has private enterprise, properly so-called, been hitherto content to hold the noiseless tenor of its way along a cool and sequestered vale, without venturing either to scale even the unambitious heights of banking or tea cultivation, or to descend to the depth of riverine steam navigation until after Government had given a lead in those directions, but that municipal assistance, on which the central Government may almost everywhere else more or less rely, has also been altogether wanting. Village communities, indeed, had existed immemorially, but centuries of alternating tyranny and anarchy had pretty nearly extinguished whatever public spirit may once have animated them. Here and there a local community might combine to prevent an ancestral tank or embankment from falling into utter ruin, but that was about the boldest stretch of their associative capacity. If left to themselves, the country people would have continued to jolt along, like their forefathers, on wheels axle-deep in sand or mud, according to the season; to see their crops burnt up to nothing when the rains failed, or swept away by torrents when the rivers were in flood; perishing themselves periodically by thousands and hundreds of thousands—in this district from starvation consequent on drought, in that from pestilence exhaled by waterlogged swamps. Clear it was on the inauguration of British rule in India that, if public works were to be, the creative fiat must proceed from the rulers.

Now in India, as elsewhere, public works may, irrespectively of other modes of classification, be arranged under two general heads: of those required exclusively or principally for governmental purposes; and of those which, however serviceable governmentally, subserve in still larger measure the convenience and interests of the people. Those belonging to the first division will here be passed over lightly, for there is seldom much danger of their being grossly neglected, and, as a matter of fact, the Anglo-Indian Government has not been particularly remiss in providing palatial residences for its presidents, or stately offices for the transaction of its civil business, or commodious barracks and sanataria for its troops. Our attention may be more profitably bestowed on works of popular utility, and among these are two subdivisions, those of Communications and Irrigation Works, each of which well merits a chapter to itself.

CHAPTER II.

COMMUNICATIONS.

UNDER this term, in the language of the Indian Public Works Department, are grouped roads, navigable canals or rivers, bridges, railways, and whatever other appliances of a permanent character have been supplied by nature or created or improved by art as aids to the locomotion and transport of passengers and goods. Among objects of governmental solicitude, there would seem to be none entitled to take precedence of these, since where these are altogether wanting it is impossible for a Government satisfactorily to discharge any of its duties, not even the primary one of protecting life and property. They are the constituents of an arterial system, without which administrative energy cannot be properly directed or distributed, and the absence of which therefore almost necessarily implies a state of things more or less approaching to anarchy.

It is not, however, so much from this point of view as from that of their popular utility, that they will now be regarded. What especially renders human beings interdependent, and constrains them to gather together into communities, is division of labour, or separation of employments. A family that does not produce for itself all the necessaries of life cannot subsist without exchanges, but for exchange there must be carriage, and for carriage some sort of landways or waterways. Of these fortunately no country is ever left absolutely destitute by nature, but it is only in proportion as they are multiplied or improved by art, that civilisation, in its earlier stages, can make very sensible progress. To the civilised rulers, then, of a backward territory, a grand opportunity is open; an opportunity of which the old Romans were always prompt to avail themselves. Of those sagacious pioneers of material progress the first care after entering Spain, Gaul, Germany, or Britain, was to cast over the land a network of roads, devised primarily for the passage of their legions, but along which the arts of peace promptly followed in the track of war, raising the social condition of the aborigines nearer and nearer to the Roman level. Neither are the English in India justly chargeable with remissness in this particular. They, too, have shown themselves, in person or by proxy, 'labouring pioneers' of the type described in 'Paradise Regained:'

> A multitude with spades and axes armed
> To lay hills plain, fell woods, or valleys fill:
> Or where plain was raise hill, or overlay
> With bridges rivers proud, as with a yoke.

They found India, a century ago, as trackless as Britain was before the Roman invasion; they have now rendered it in most directions as permeable as England was in the early part of the Georgian era, when as yet only one stage coach a month oscillated between

London and Edinburgh, and that one was usually a fortnight on the way, and while it was only 'God willing' that a coach-proprietor would promise to convey passengers from London to Exeter or Nottingham in so few as four days and four nights. In India, however, as elsewhere, the national appetite for locomotive appliances has grown with what it has fed on: increase of supply has begotten increase of demand. Every newly-opened route has become parent of a traffic requiring subsidiary routes for its accommodation : insomuch that the Government, aghast at such ever-multiplying claims on its resources, is anxiously casting about for auxiliaries to whom to delegate part of the obligation of meeting the requisitions. This it may do without any dereliction of duty or departure from the salutary principles insisted on in our first chapter, for, as has been said, every large community is an aggregate of smaller ones; there are everywhere publics within publics—communal and urban clustering into cantonal, cantonal into provincial, provincial into national—and it is generally the reverse of desirable that the central authority should continue to do aught which the local authorities can contrive to do at all passably. So of late years, some of the wisest of Anglo-Indian statesmen have been endeavouring to establish or to resuscitate institutions more or less analogous to the parish vestries, civic corporations, and county sessions of their native land. 'I have always,' says Sir George Campbell, 'believed that while, on the one hand, the task of really governing India down to the villages and the people is too great for the British Government, and, on the other, anything like national political freedom is inconsistent with a foreign rule, we may best supplement our own deficiencies and give the people that measure of self-government and local freedom to which both their old traditions and their modern education alike point, by giving to towns and restoring to villages some sort of municipal or communal self-government.'[1] These sentiments of Sir George Campbell are shared by other equally exalted functionaries, and as under his auspices in the Central Provinces and in Bengal, so also in the Presidencies of Madras and Bombay, in the North-West Provinces, and signally, under the fostering tutelage of Sir Robert Montgomery, in the Punjab, the germs of municipal organisation have been, or are being gradually developed. Here and there, both in town and country, committees have been created, and vested with powers of local taxation for local purposes, and on them, in proportion as they become qualified for the work, the charge of the vicinal roads devolves. The function will afford them abundant occupation, but for its proper discharge it is desirable that more attention than they have hitherto received should be given to some rather obvious considerations. It might be well to begin by tracing out beforehand, as completely as may be, a comprehensive scheme of the roads likely to be required, advertence being had to any projected railways to which the roads might serve as feeders : otherwise there will be consider-

[1] Report on Administration of Bengal, 1871–72, p. 192.

able risk of thoroughfares, constructed at a cost which can ill be spared, being before long superseded, and falling as completely into disuse as portions of our own Great North Road, on which grass now grows where once cart and coach wheels were perpetually grinding. Then, inasmuch as it must generally be better that one set of travellers or traders should be enabled to get quite to their journey's end than that two or more sets should be stopped midway by insurmountable obstacles, it would also be better that no more roads should be commenced at one time than there were means of finishing off-hand. Not unfrequently, too, it might not be amiss to reverse the usual plan of marking the terrene sections of a road first, and leaving the bridges to be added later, since the most excellent macadamisation can but imperfectly answer its purpose if broken in its course at every few miles by a deep gully or broad river or rapid torrent, whereas, but for these interruptions, hackery drivers would have little difficulty in improvising a variety of tracks over the wide stretches of open plain of which so much of India consists. Another point particularly to be borne in mind, in circles betraying a tendency to railway mania, is that common roads are not so much the proper supplements of railways as railways are of common roads, and that it can only be where local conditions are very exceptional that railways are entitled to precedence. This is a point to which we may probably have occasion to recur.

That

> Experience ever till too late defers
> Her captious counsel, while the wariest errs
> For lack of guidance,

is a reflection very likely to occur to any one who calmly reviews the history of Indian railways, in regard to which the policy originally adopted, and until recently persisted in, is not the less objectionable for having been the result of much anxious deliberation. The basis of this policy was a Minute drawn up in 1853 by the late Marquis Dalhousie, then Governor-General, in which several questions bearing upon the grand issue are discussed with characteristic ability. The advantages, political, social, and commercial, that might be expected to accrue to India from a national network of railways are eloquently set forth; the principal outlines of such a network are marked; certain principles of construction are laid down; and a special agency indicated as that to which construction might be most expediently entrusted. The Marquis was emphatically a man of commanding intellect. Not only was he much in the habit of laying down the law: he had also a way of causing that law to be very generally accepted as gospel. So powerful was his impress on those who came closely into contact with him that, even at this distance of time, it is, with many eminent men brought up in his school, a sufficient recommendation of any part of Lord Dalhousie's policy to be able to say that it was Lord Dalhousie's.

Doubtless this personal influence was, in a great measure, deserved, for to get one's familiars to believe in one's superiority is always a proof of real superiority of some sort. It is a pity, however, that respect for authority should ever go so far as to paralyse private judgment; and it is a pity that Lord Dalhousie's Railway

Minute should, by reason of its authorship. have been exempted from early criticism. The doctrine of that famous State Paper bears upon the surface full evidence of having been carefully thought out by his Lordship himself, but if other independent thinkers had been at hand to take part in the process, it is not impossible that warning might have been given and taken betimes against two grievous defects in his Lordship's programme.

For the first and greatest of these, there was, it may be admitted, considerable excuse. When the ruling powers had resolved that Indian railways should be, there was no possibility of inducing private capitalists to accept the risk of creating them. Indian capitalists, as a rule, adventure nothing without what they believe to be full security for at least 12 per cent. profit; and English capitalists had a recollection too rueful and too recent of the bursting of railway bubbles at home to have much fancy for exposing their remaining substance to the chance of being converted into similar airy nothings abroad. Private enterprise, therefore, properly so-called—the courage, that is, that discreetly confronts danger, not the timidity that insists on being protected against the bare possibility of its occurrence—was out of the question. If India was to have railways, there were practically but two ways in which she could be provided with them. Either Government might take their construction into its own hands, employing therein either its own officers or contractors under direct engagements with itself, or it might induce bodies of shareholders to undertake the preliminaries and superintendence of construction by ensuring them against all risk from the undertaking: in other words, it might institute guaranteed railway companies. Of these alternatives, Lord Dalhousie deliberately decided in favour of the second, guided in his preference, as he explains, by reasons negative and positive. The negative, consisting partly of stock objections to governmental action in commercial undertakings of any kind, partly of special objections to that action in undertakings of this peculiar kind, have already been sufficiently discussed. The most important of the positive was a peculiar capacity with which the guaranteed companies were somewhat gratuitously credited for introducing into India English capital and English skill and energy. His Lordship was aware that the advantages of the guarantee system, whatever they might be, would be attended by their own peculiar drawbacks, and in particular, might not be procurable without some sacrifice, both of economy and speed. He was persuaded, however, that the sacrifice would be insignificant. He did not apprehend that the companies would get on with their work much more slowly than Government would have done in their place; and although their work might probably enough be somewhat more expensive, still he calculated that the ordinary cost of railway construction under their management would approximate to 5,000*l.* a mile, and that even where extraordinary difficulties were to be encountered the maximum cost would not exceed 8,500*l.* a mile. Such were Lord Dalhousie's vaticinations, with which it may be edifying to contrast, as we shall presently have occasion to do, actual realisations.

In justice, however, it must be explained that although the original germ of the guarantee system was of Lord Dalhousie's conception, the responsibility for its subsequently luxuriant development belongs to others. He would have been one of the last to put forward proposals for the guarantee, pure and simple, of interest on all capital applied to railway construction. His recommendations in that direction were qualified by some very material conditions. He distinctly stipulated, firstly, that the guarantee should be restricted to such amount as carefully-prepared estimates should show to be presumably indispensable for the work to be done; and, secondly, that the guarantee should be partially withdrawn in the event of the work not being completed within a prescribed period. If these precautions had been observed, they could not indeed have endowed the guarantee system with any positive virtue, but they might at any rate have gone far towards freeing it from the worst of its many vices. Unfortunately the prudential part of Lord Dalhousie's counsel was entirely neglected. Governor-General though he was, he was not himself competent to inaugurate the order of things he contemplated, but was bound to submit it for sanction to his superiors at home—in those days the Court of Directors of the East Indian Company. Now far be it from me, in speaking of that august body, to fall short in the smallest measure of the respect due to departed greatness. Among its members were several of strong sense and clear vision, well fitted to sit in judgment on the proposals of their Lord Deputy. Collectively, however, they were under an immense disadvantage in comparison with their exalted nominee. His was one master mind, while their minds, whatever their quality, were in number many, and *quot homines, tot sententiæ*; for many heterogeneous minds to coalesce in any homogeneous sentiment is among the rarest phenomena of psychical chemistry. The conclusion they arrive at is always either the result of an interchange of compromises, representing everybody's scruples and nobody's convictions, or it is acquiesced in out of sheer weariness and exhaustion after the discordant debaters have grown so sick of the subject that they will agree to anything in order to get rid of it. The second of these courses was probably the one taken on the occasion in question, for on no other supposition is it easy to understand how the Court of Directors could have eliminated all the best parts of Lord Dalhousie's scheme, retaining all the bad, and introducing novelties of their own devising worse than anything in the original. The guarantee they finally resolved upon was practically unlimited. Under the contracts entered into by them with the companies which they called into existence, if the first estimate for a railway should subsequently prove insufficient, it might be doubled or trebled, little choice being reserved to Government but that of guaranteeing whatever amounts might successively be demanded for the completion of the undertaking, for any period, however protracted, over which its construction might be extended. Wise after the event, any one may now perceive the inevitable tendency of such arrangements. If it had been desired to make the Railway Boards extravagant, what more certain mode could have been adopted than that of securing to them the full current rate of interest on whatever sums they might expend? Certainly, if such was the desire, it has been amply gratified. It took the guaranteed companies twenty years to make 5,300 miles of railway, that is to say, they made on an average 265 miles annually. During the same period their total expenditure was ninety millions sterling, or on an average 17,000*l.* per mile. On one line the average cost has exceeded 23,000*l.* a mile. On three only, the Madras, Great Southern of India, and Oude and Rohilcund, has it been so low as 10,000*l.* And this expenditure is simply for bare construction and for rolling stock. It is exclusive of unearned interest on capital; exclusive, too, of the value of the land occupied, which in India is furnished gratis by Government, and it has not been inordinately swollen by legal expenses, for there has been little local opposition or interested rivalry to overcome. Yet, though free from some of the items which figure most conspicuously in the capital accounts of English lines, with every acre of land given free, with no parliamentary battles and no battle of the gauges to fight, railway construction in India during the first twenty years averaged 17,000*l.* a mile, or just double Lord Dalhousie's highest estimate.

The Indian guarantee system has now, thanks to Lords Lawrence and Mayo and the Duke of Argyll, become so thoroughly discredited, that to dwell heavily on its manifold enormities might seem almost ungenerous. The amazing self-contradictions and onesidedness of the contracts by which the reciprocal engagements of the guaranteeing Government and of the guaranteed Companies are defined shall therefore be passed over very lightly. How in one clause of each of those remarkable indentures it is provided that at the end of a 99 years' lease the railway treated of shall by mere fluxion of time pass absolutely and gratuitously into the Government's possession, and how by the very next clause the proprietary Company, if preferring to be paid for the line and its appurtenances instead of parting with them for nothing, is empowered to exact from Government their full cost price; how in one place the contracts reserve to Government the right of disallowing any expenditure incurred without its sanction, while in another the governmental guarantee of interest is virtually extended to all expenditure, whether sanctioned or not; how the Government has pledged itself, in the event of its desiring to purchase a prosperous railway before the expiration of the lease, to pay the full market value, yet has equally pledged itself, however loth to purchase, to pay, on demand, for a line that cannot earn even its working expenses, every penny that may have been wasted on so utter a failure; how, in short, as if deliberately adopting as motto, 'Heads you win, tails I lose,' it has bound itself by formal deed to accept every possible loss, and to forego any possibility of gain—is not all this and more of the same sort written in the Blue Books of the Parliamentary Committee on Indian Finance?

The other grave defect of the Dalhousian programme is the choice of the 5 ft. 6 in. gauge. This perhaps may have been adopted as a compromise between the English 7 ft. and 4 ft. 8½ in. gauges, whose internecine strife was then at its height. Such at least was more probably the reason for the selection than the only other which I have heard suggested, viz. fear that trains of carriages adapted to a narrower gauge might not be proof against the fury of an Indian hurricane, but would be liable to be overthrown and swept away like chaff by abnormal blasts. It is so difficult to believe that one of the most circumspect of her Governors-General can have deliberately saddled India for all time to come with an annual charge of at least a quarter of a million sterling for the sake of such inadequate protection against so improbable a danger, that this explanation may be summarily dismissed. Still, whether desire of compromise or whatever else may have been Lord Dalhousie's motive, that motive was certainly allowed to operate with total disregard of what ought really to have been the determining considerations. Among these there are two of superlative importance. Plainly there can be no such thing as a gauge intrinsically the best and universally the most appropriate. Plainly, the first condition to be regarded is the maximum of prospective traffic, and this having been duly calculated, the next is the size of vehicle by which stowage for the expected traffic can be most conveniently afforded—the consideration of this second condition of course embracing that of the gauge most suitable for the economical construction of machinery capable of coping with the resistance to be overcome. Given a certain amount of traffic, the best size of vehicle is plainly that within which the traffic may be readily accommodated with least waste of space. No doubt if there be bulk enough to load a broad-wheeled wagon, the wagon is greatly to be preferred to a hand-barrow; but if, on the other hand, there be altogether only some few barrow-loads, the barrow is as indubitably to be preferred to the wagon. Now as the actual traffic of English railways averages nearly 27,000 passengers and 12,000 tons of goods per mile, while that of India averages less than 4,000 passengers and 700 tons, it may be confidently predicted that the future Indian average will not rise above the actual English during the lifetime of many successive generations of rails. But as, for the actual English traffic, vehicles from 7 ft. 6 in. to 9 ft. wide have been proved by ample experience to be amply sufficient, it follows that the same width would suffice even for the prospective traffic of Indian lines, and that it is so is virtually acknowledged by the companies to whom the Indian guaranteed lines belong, and by whom they are worked, and who on their gauge of 5 ft. 6 in. are content to place rolling stock as nearly as may be of the same dimensions as those considered most suitable to the English gauge of 4 ft. 8½ in. But it is statistically demonstrable that these dimensions are not simply equal to, but largely in excess of Indian prospective necessities. Wherever—which in this matter is but another word for everywhere—wherever the exigencies of railway traffic require rapid delivery at stations intermediate as well as terminal, it is impossible to wait until trains are anything like fully laden before despatching them, and, as a matter of fact, the average quantity and weight of goods and number of passengers carried in railway wagons and carriages is everywhere far below the carrying capacity of the vehicles.

On the best worked lines in America, cars built to carry 10 tons carry on an average only 2·7 tons, and even in France, where railway managers, being comparatively free from competition, fill the carriages as full as they can, the proportion of available passenger seats actually occupied is on the six principal lines only 0·240, while on the same lines the coal and coke trucks and ordinary goods wagons, though built to carry 10, carry less than 5 tons. In the United Kingdom, where competition is keener than elsewhere, the average loads bear a still smaller proportion to capacity, the paying weight being to dead weight only as 1 to 7 in respect to goods, and only as 1 to 29 in respect to passengers.[1] But the carrying capacity of English vehicles, being thus very greatly more than double what is absolutely requisite for stowage of the total quantity of goods and accommodation of the total number of passengers, might surely be reduced by about one-sixth, and yet remain sufficient for all practical purposes. If the vehicles, instead of averaging 8 ft., were only 6½ ft. wide, they would still be generally started with very much less than their full loads. Vehicles of 6½ ft. width would therefore abundantly suffice for actual English traffic, and if for actual English, then also for Indian prospective; and consequently a sufficing Indian gauge would be the narrowest to which rolling stock of 6½ ft. width could be conveniently adapted.

[1] Railways or no Railways, by Robert F. Fairlie, pp. 41–43.

Now on various lines—Belgian, Swedish, Norwegian, and American—of gauges ranging from 3 to 3½ ft., rolling stock 6½ ft. wide and upwards has long been in use with triumphant success. Presumably, then, a 3 ft. 6 in. gauge would have sufficed for India, and the whole difference of cost between that gauge and 5 ft. 6 in. has consequently been at best utterly thrown away. There are, indeed, spirits bold enough to argue that there is no difference in cost between the two—nay, that, if there be any difference, it is in favour of the broader gauge; but the courage which rises to the level of this thesis would probably not shrink from maintaining that a broad-wheeled wagon costs less to build than a dog-cart. Faith so intrepid and so earnest is not to be argued with, for e'en though vanquished it will argue still, and it deserves besides to be left in possession of its own honest convictions; but to advocates of less resolution it must surely be self-evident that where less earthwork, shorter and [1] slenderer sleepers and lighter rails will suffice, and where recourse may be had to sharper curves and steeper gradients, which, besides straightening and shortening the line, allow much costly excavation and costlier tunnelling to

[1] The difference of price between large and small sleepers is much more than proportionate to the difference of scantling. 'The same merchants,' says Mr. Fairlie, 'are supplying me with sleepers for a 4 ft. 8½ in. line at the rate of 2*s.* 8*d.* per sleeper, and with others of exactly similar quality for a 3 ft. 6 in. line at 10*d.* each. The reason of this is of course because the larger scantlings cut to waste, while the others can be produced out of smaller, and consequently cheaper, timber. On a mile of average single track are 2.112 ties, which at 2*s.* 8*d.* would cost 281*l.* 12*s.*; at 10*d.*, 88*l.*'—Fairlie's Railways or no Railways, p. 29.

be dispensed with, *some* saving must be practicable. How much that saving may be is no doubt a different question, and one indeed as to which experts differ to an extent scarcely creditable to their expertness.

In the hot debate on the subject, which occupied seven consecutive meetings of the Institution of Civil Engineers, and in which most of the English magnates of the profession took part, personally or by proxy, the amount of saving was, on the authority of Mr. John Fowler, stated at 866*l.*, and on that of Sir John Hawkshaw, at 760*l.* per mile, while, upon data furnished by one or other of these gentlemen, it was by a third hand calculated at 1,000*l.* By Mr. Bidder it was reduced to 600*l.* per mile, and by Mr. Harrison to 400*l.*, while by Mr. Bruce even 200*l.* was only grudgingly conceded. Such and so wide being the disagreement between doctors of the profession, unlearned non-professionals may be excused if the inference thence drawn by them be that theoretical speculation is here out of its depth, and that certainty can be approached only by the path of experiment. Fortunately that path has already been to some extent opened. The Indian Government, actuated by motives which may readily be guessed, and which shall presently be explained, has within the last few years undertaken the construction of some hundreds of miles of railway on a gauge as narrow as the French metre, or 3 ft. 3⅜ in.; and, whereas the cost of the 5 ft. 6 in. lines of the guaranteed companies has averaged 17,000*l.* per mile, and has in one instance been as high as 20,000*l.*, the highest cost of those sections of the metre lines which have as yet been opened, has in no instance exceeded 6,000*l.* per mile. Of course, the whole of the difference thus shown is not attributable to difference of gauge; in all probability to the superior economy of Government agency a larger portion of credit is due; but still, after the largest deduction on this account that can conscientiously be claimed, the residue attributable to gauge will be very considerable, certainly not less than 1,000*l.* per mile. At that rate, the first 5,000 miles of railway constructed in India must have cost five millions more than they would have done if made on the metre instead of the 5 ft. 6 in. gauge. And the proportion of the cost of construction which might thus have been saved would be of comparatively small account if it had simply been wasted, simply thrown away, and if, unfortunately, the waste in the first instance did not necessitate corresponding perennial waste thereafter. But needlessly broad gauge occasions employment of needlessly capacious and heavy wagons and carriages, requiring for haulage proportionably more powerful and heavier locomotives, which again consume proportionably more of that fearful item, fuel. The extra weight of rolling stock causes greater friction along the rails, and greater wear and tear both of rails and rolling stock, the extra expense of repairing which, and of repairs in general, observes of course a tolerably exact ratio to extra original cost. Thus the original waste of five millions on construction has saddled the railways with an extra annual expenditure, which, if capitalised, would assuredly represent at least five millions more. These calculations too, be it noted, have proceeded on the assumption that the same principles of equipment must be adopted on all gauges, and have avoided all reference to the possibility of adapting to metre gauge lines certain ingenious novelties in rolling stock which are commonly held to be inapplicable to lines of much greater and much wider gauge. Here, however, I am approaching delicate ground. Even by the untechnical looker-on a modest tribute of admiration might perhaps be not unbecomingly paid to the remarkable ability with which the Fairlie theory has been advocated by its author; but valour's better part, discretion, will be best evinced by my steering altogether clear of a contest in which the most eminent of technical adepts are so apt to lose their heads as well as their tempers.

From an enumeration of the defects of the Dalhousian system the conflict of authority which it involves must not be omitted. The perhaps necessary, but necessarily irritating interference of Government in petty details, the perverse recalcitrance which such interference naturally engenders, and the consequent impossibility of obtaining the most obvious improvements except as the result of prolonged wrangling—these things no doubt contributed largely to the exasperation felt by some recent occupants of Lord Dalhousie's exalted office against the railway policy which his Lordship had transmitted to them as a baleful heirloom, and by the continual provocations of which the righteous soul of Lord Lawrence in especial seems to have been sorely vexed. To that downright, straightforward temper of his, which, when a public object is in view, aims straight at it without overmuch tenderness for any individual feelings or interests that chance to stand in the way, it must have been singularly galling to be compelled to remain a passive spectator of the constant misapplication of national resources inseparable from extension of the guarantee system. Accordingly, as appears from correspondence of his with the Home Government, printed by order of the House of Commons, he was throughout his term of Viceroyalty incessant in denunciations of a state of things productive of such mischievous consequences, and by his immediate successor, the Earl of Mayo, the same strain was taken up and continued with genuine Hibernian fervour. The complaints of both met with sympathising audience in their respectively contemporary Secretaries of State, Sir Stafford Northcote, and the Duke of Argyll. To the last-named minister, who went with especial heartiness into Indian railway reform, the question at issue presented itself in the following shape. To the guaranteed companies had been entrusted the construction of about five thousand miles of railway, whereof about four thousand had been completed—these had on an average cost 17,000*l.* a mile, or about seventy millions altogether; to complete the five thousand at the same rate would raise the aggregate cost to about ninety millions sterling. According to the most recent data the completed mileage was yielding a net annual revenue of 2,200,000*l.*, while the annual interest for which Government was responsible was 3,700,000*l.*, the amount which it had annually to make good being therefore 1,500,000*l.*, to be raised, not impossibly, to nearly 2,000,000*l.* by the time the companies' lines were finished. But in order that India should have anything like her fair complement of railways, fully 10,000 miles would have to be added to the 5,000 already in a manner provided for, and to construct these 10,000 by means of the same agency and on the same scale, was a prospect which no Indian financier could contemplate without affright. Extension of the guarantee system was therefore not to be thought of, yet on the other hand there was no hope of self-styled private enterprise coming forward without a guarantee. Capitalists had become at once downhearted and demoralised in regard to Indian railways. The achievements of the guaranteed companies had dispelled the prestige which once attached to those investments. The glittering possibilities of 10 or 20 per cent. of net earnings, which had once encircled them like a halo, dazzling the eyes of primitive subscribers, had been displaced by realisations of 2 or 3, or at most of 5 per cent., and even if this last rate could have been safely reckoned upon, it would have lost much of its attraction for those who, by purchasing guaranteed stock at the current market price, could make perfectly sure of nearly the same interest. Thus Government had practically no alternative but to take into its own hands the business of further railway extension. It had now forced upon it what would from the beginning have been its wisest course. Nor was this the only change of plan that had now become virtually a necessity. The utmost economy to be expected from the adoption of State agency could scarcely be expected to suffice to make the projected railways remunerative. The best ground was already occupied by the guaranteed companies, and, of the country remaining to be traversed by the State lines, part was so nearly desert that without powerful political and strategical reasons to reinforce the feeble commercial inducements, there would have been no justification for allowing it to be so traversed at all, while in scarcely any part was there early prospect of more than very moderate commercial traffic. To make the State lines on a scale which experience had shown to be ruinously magnificent, would therefore have been an aggravated blunder, and the expediency of a considerable reduction of gauge followed as a matter of course. Such were in substance the recommendations which Lord Mayo, following closely in the path chalked out by Lord Lawrence, placed before the Duke of Argyll, and to which His Grace assented with the less hesitation from having been already favourably disposed towards them by independent investigation of the pros and cons. Accordingly, it was presently resolved that the construction of fresh railways should thenceforth be a State affair, and also that on the State lines the width of gauge should be the French metre, or 3 ft. 3⅜ in. A good deal of preparation, however, was necessary before much visible effect could be given to the resolution. Establishments had to be organised, tracts of country surveyed, designs, estimates, and specifications prepared, so that it was not till the autumn of 1870 that field operations fairly commenced. Reasonable progress has since been made.

On the map prefixed to this volume is sketched, with

as much correctness as is at present possible, the Indian system of railways, existing and prospective, the portions already executed being distinguished from those under construction, and these again from those which have not yet advanced beyond the survey stage; the broad and narrow gauge likewise being separately indicated. It will be seen that from Calcutta emerge two trunk lines, one in a north-easterly direction, until stopped at Goalundo by the appalling difficulty of bridging the Brahmaputra, but, before arriving there, throwing off, due north from Khoostea, a vertical shoot which is intended to reach nearly to Darjeeling at the foot of the Himalayas, and which some time or other will no doubt branch out laterally deep into Assam; the other, running westward from Calcutta, through Allahabad, Delhi, Agra, and Lahore towards Peshawur, and having on the north, for 500 or 600 miles of its course, a quasi-parallel line through Oude and Rohilcund. A third trunk line, commencing at Lahore, descends to Mooltan, and thence down the valley of the Indus to the port of Kurrachee. Bombay is the starting point of what, without reference to their ownership, may be regarded as three distinct railways—one running northwards to Ahmedabad, where it throws off two short westerly branches, and whence it will ere long be extended, through the heart of Rajpootana, to Delhi and Agra; a second trending to the north-east for about 350 miles, and then trifurcating, on the left to Indore and towards Ajmeer, straight onward through Jubbulpore to Allahabad, and on the left to Nagpore and towards

Raipore and Cuttack; and a third which, by a south-easterly course, connects Bombay with Madras, and from which lateral branches will place both cities in communication with the Nizam's capital, Hydrabad, and with the cotton fields of Dharwar and the port of Carwar. At Madras commences a southern sub-system, whose other terminal points are or will be Beypore, and, it is to be hoped, Cochin on the Malabar coast, Cuddalore, Negapatam, and Tuticorin on the Coromandel coast, and Mysore inland.

When this programme is fully worked out, India will be traversed latitudinally, from side to side and from sea to sea, by some half-dozen of what, without excessive looseness of speech, may be termed quasi-parallel lines of iron way—from Calcutta through Lucknow and Lahore, or through Allahabad, Agra, Delhi, and Lahore to Peshawur, and likewise to Kurrachee ; from Calcutta to Bombay ; from Bombay to the apex of the Mahanuddy Delta, and also to Madras ; from Madras to Carwar and also to Beypore ; and from Beypore to Negapatam ; while from the feet of the Himalayas at Peshawur, Darjeeling, and some point in easternmost Assam, will descend *en zigzag* longitudinal lines which, uniting at Bombay, will proceed thence to Tuticorin, within a few score miles of Cape Comorin, another likewise descending from Peshawur to Kurrachee. Each of the Peninsula's few seaports will be the terminus of at least one line, while towards each of the three presidential capitals three lines will converge. Within the whole length and breadth of the land, there will, in short, be no two places of prime importance from one to the other of which peaceful passengers, merchandise and troops will not be able to proceed by rail.

But although the greater part of the programme has already been executed, not only is a good deal still wanting to complete it, but two of its sections, the one from Carwar into the interior, and the extension eastwards from Nagpore, have not been as yet definitely decided upon. Of these, the former, after having for some time been regarded with especial favour in influential quarters, has of late fallen into discredit. The chief advantage to be expected from it is that of affording greatly increased facilities of export to the produce of the countries beyond the Ghauts. There, over an area of 3,800 square miles, stretch the fertile plains of Dharwar, a district noted for its cotton, and not merely for the indigenous, but also for the American, species, which was introduced some 30 years ago, and is now cultivated with considerable success. For that and all other exports the chief places of shipment were until lately five open roadsteads, Akola, Coompta, Honore, Rutnagherry, and Vingorla, little use being made of Carwar, whose small but convenient and sheltered harbour, though in the last century the site of a factory of the East India Company, fell subsequently into such neglect and oblivion that it may almost be said to have been rediscovered when, in the year 1857, attention was again drawn to it by Lieut. Taylor, of the Indian Navy. Since then a good cart road has been made over the mountain barrier which everywhere intervenes between

Dharwar and the sea, but the superiority of this new route has not as yet had much effect in diverting trade from its accustomed channels, and, of the pack bullocks and bullock hackeries that pass from the interior to the coast, the greater number are still led by tracks, little better than bridle-paths, to Coompta, whence their freight is conveyed by small craft to Bombay, to be there tran-shipped for final conveyance to Europe. No doubt all this would be materially changed if rails were laid down from Carwar for a sufficient distance inland, but recent inquiries have resulted in grave apprehension that the traffic attracted by the supposed iron way would not suffice to make it pay. Let us assume, for the moment and for the sake of argument, that this apprehension is well founded, and that, therefore, the undertaking in question cannot commend itself to private enterprise; still it is by no means necessarily one in which the Government, as representing the entire public, might not very advantageously engage. It would possess in large measure the sort of utility referred to in the preceding chapter. According to very careful computation, a railway 145 miles long from Carwar to Gudduck would cost 1,100,000*l.*; if extended 90 miles further to Bellary, its cost would be increased to 1,595,000*l.* On these sums, if borrowed, as in the present state of the Indian Government's credit they might be, at 4 per cent., interest upon them would amount to 44,000*l.* and 63,800*l.* respectively. Now, no one supposes that the railway would earn absolutely no net revenue. Even though it did no better than the least successful of the existing guaranteed lines, it would earn nearly 1 per cent. net, while if it did as well as any except the least successful of the same lines, it would net 2½ per cent. on its cost. But irrespectively of any such direct returns, there is good reason to expect that, regarded from a national point of view, its indirect advantages would of themselves be abundant money's worth for the money spent. Let us pause here to consider once again what the indirect advantages of railway communication are. Not only are old markets made more cheaply accessible, access to new markets afforded, and production stimulated by enlarged demand for its fruits, but capital in search of investment discovers fresh fields, and producers are placed in possession of better implements and made acquainted with better processes. Together with the passengers whom they carry about, railways distribute also certain impalpable entities—observation, intelligence, invention, technical skill, and miscellaneous information—distributing them moreover carriage free. Even in England, people who in the old stage-coach days would never have gone ten miles beyond the nearest market town in the whole course of their lives, are now tempted every now and then to make long journeys by rail: how certainly then would similar temptation set the same sort of people similarly in motion in a country where dawk bearers or bullock carts had previously been the speediest and easiest means of conveyance. While so journeying, a farmer from a backward district cannot look out of his own compartment window without noticing better modes of cultivation than he has previously been familiar with, and an artist or mechanic on a visit to a manufacturing town is equally likely to pick up useful hints about his business. On their return home some of these persons put in practice the superior processes of which they have taken note; while, on the other hand, the technical expert, who, when first traversing a neglected tract, had spied out unsuspected seeds of wealth sprinkled over the nakedness of the land, would not improbably return thither with the requisite appliances for developing its resources, for clothing its wastes with luxuriant crops, quarrying its mines, and utilising its water power. Dharwar and the adjoining provinces would be singularly unlucky if causes like these did not operate there, as elsewhere, after the construction of the projected railway allowed of their being brought to bear. Foremost among the staple products is cotton, the culture of which in Dharwar occupies more than half a million of acres, or not much less than a third of the whole cultivated area: the indigenous plant being grown on 300,000 out of the half million of acres, and the New Orleans or other exotic varieties on the remaining 200,000. What room for improvement there is in the local modes of cultivation may be judged of from the fact that, whereas in India generally the average yield per acre of cotton is seventy-three pounds, in Dharwar it is only twenty-four, the produce of the New Orleans plant being nevertheless two or three times as great as that of the indigenous. Wherefore, even though adoption of Carwar instead of Bombay as the ultimate port of shipment for Europe, should have no further effect than that of leading to the general substitution of New Orleans for indigenous cotton in local cultivation, and of raising the local yield per acre to the general average of India, an addition of more than twenty-four millions of pounds would be made to the total annual yield; and it is but charitable to assume that some of the mercantile houses of Bombay would be enterprising enough to depute agents to settle down at Carwar, or at Hooblee or other places in the interior, and bestir themselves to bring about these improvements, or that if they were not, some of Liverpool and Manchester would. When Lancashire and Dharwar were perceived to be within a month's easy reach of each other, Lancashire would scarcely fail to supply Bombay's neglect. Nor would the supposed improvements be necessarily limited to cotton: corn, rice, pulse, oil-seed, sugar, and tobacco each in its degree, would no doubt proportionably benefit, the entire agricultural produce of the province being thus augmented by something like a third. The annual increase of national wealth which all this implies would be equivalent to very many times 50,000*l.*, so that, in the capacity of trustee for the nation, Government would plainly be making a most excellent investment of national wealth by annually employing in the manner supposed the amount of capital represented by 50,000*l.* of annual interest. Nor in that capacity only: the share of the general increase that would find its way into the Government treasury would amply suffice to make the railway indirectly remunerative. For the cultivators, when enabled to obtain so much more from the soil than previously, would be able to pay higher rents for their holdings, and the addition of only eightpence per acre to the present assessment would, independently of the contemporaneous increase reasonably to be expected from the salt, customs, excise, and miscellaneous sources of revenue, amount to precisely 50,000*l.*

A similar, though not quite so strong a case, may be made out in favour of an extension of railway communication eastward from Nagpore, through the district of Bundara and into the heart of Chutteesgurh, continuable thence either to Calcutta, or through Raipore and Sumbulpore to Cuttack. There are but slight grounds for supposing that this line, if constructed, would pay directly, or until after a pretty long interval. Mr. Morris, indeed, who has for some years been Chief Commissioner of the Central Provinces, reckoned at one time that it would pay immediately if it could be constructed for 2,700*l.* a mile, but subsequent estimates have raised the expected cost to 4,200*l.* a mile, at which rate the traffic that would hardly pay on 2,700*l.* would leave a yearly loss of at least 60*l.* a mile, or of 80,000*l.* altogether, on the cost of 130 miles between Nagpore and Dongagurh, at which latter place it is proposed that the railway should in the first instance terminate. But against the direct loss are to be set off certain indirect gains which are thus summed up by Mr. Morris:—

'The people of the Nagpore country draw part of their food supply from Chutteesgurh, but as the communications are difficult and expensive,' averaging 4½*d.* per ton per mile by country cart or pack bullock, 'they are obliged to grow a great deal of food for themselves, and are thus prevented from growing a great breadth of cotton, which is their most lucrative crop. The people of the Chutteesgurh and Bundara country have an enormous surplus of food produce, which must go to Nagpore for a market, and part of which, for want of a market, is sometimes left to rot in the stacks. But the cost of sending this surplus to Nagpore is at least four times as great as it ought to be if there were railway communication, the time occupied being moreover as many days as it would then be hours. And, in consequence, the producers of the eastern districts get a much lower price for their surplus grain, while the consumers of the western districts pay a much higher price for their food than they would if the grain trade from Raipore to Nagpore, which already in the year 1868–9 amounted to 34,545 tons, went by railway.'

Now, surrounding the city of Nagpore, are about 7,000 square miles of black soil, almost all of which is capable of growing cotton; but of these 7,000 miles only about 3,000 are actually cultivated, and, of these again, not more than 800 are under cotton, the remaining 2,200 being for the most part occupied with food grains. Of Chutteesgurh, the total area is 18,000 miles, the cultivated area, 5,000, almost entirely under food grain or oil-seed. If Mr. Morris be right in supposing that the substitution of railway for country cart or pack bullock would bring down the cost of carriage of grain between Chutteesgurh and Nagpore from 4½*d.* to a penny per ton per mile, diminishing it, that is, by three-fourths, it seems certain that, in the Nagpore market, home-grown grain would no longer be able to compete with that of Chutteesgurh: that in the

Nagpore country 2,200 additional square miles would become available for cotton culture, and that a simultaneously increased demand for imported grain in the Nagpore market would enable a larger additional breadth of land in Chutteesgurh to be profitably sown with grain during the three months of the year which, according to Mr. Morris, are now spent by the Chutteesgurh ryots in carting their produce to Nagpore. Then, on the assumption that the yield of cotton in Nagpore is only equal to the average of India, viz. 73 lbs. per acre, or 46,720 lbs. per square mile, and its value on the spot 5*d.* per lb., there might, in the shape of cotton alone, be a fresh creation of annual wealth to the extent of about 46,080 tons, worth nearly 2,200,000*l.* Now, it being as a general principle recognised throughout India, that the Government, except where its rights have been limited by express contract, is entitled to a proportion of the net produce of the soil, regulated in part by local custom and varying accordingly, but approximating generally to one-half, it follows that at the next settlement, at the latest, the Government share of the aforesaid 2,220,000*l.* a year resulting from extended cotton culture in the Nagpore country would, together with its rent from the waste land brought under grain culture in Chutteesgurh, amount to considerably more than 80,000*l.* a year, while, even in the meantime, its miscellaneous revenue would be largely increased in consequence of the increased consumption by an enriched population of various commodities charged with excise and customs duties. Of salt, more especially, the consumption could not fail to be enormously increased when it was carried by railway into Chutteesgurh.[1]

As already intimated, the place at which it is intended that the Chutteesgurh Railway shall in the first instance terminate is Dongaghur, about 130 miles north-west of Cuttack, but the projectors of the line recommend that it be eventually extended to Calcutta, between which capital and Bombay the distance to be travelled would then, as a glance at the map will show, be reduced by not much less than a third. There are, however, grounds for believing that a preferable extension would in many respects be from Dongaghur to Cuttack. Much of the country that this portion of the line would intersect is indeed almost *terra incognita*, and presumably in so wild and backward a state, that even the powerful impulse afforded by a railway might have little immediate effect in developing its resources. There might perhaps be a good deal of through traffic destined partly for Cuttack, and partly for ulterior conveyance to the sea coast by the navigable channels of the Mahanuddy Delta; but still it is quite certain that the line would not for a very long time pay directly, and exceedingly improbable that it would pay even indirectly in ordinary years. In exceptional years, however, one in every ten or so, the good done by it might be amply sufficient to make up for all the losses of an entire previous decade. Its length might be about 350 miles, and its cost of construction not very much

[1] Salt, by being railway borne, has been rendered 40 per cent. cheaper at Nagpore than it was previously to the opening of the railway from Bombay.

less than two millions sterling. But to the Government alone, irrespectively of the indescribable misery undergone by the population at large, the cost of the Orissa famine of 1866, what with the expense of importing food by sea, remission of land revenue immediately due, and subsequent cessation of revenue from land left without cultivators, cannot have been much less than two millions, great part of which would have been saved if means had existed of bringing in food by railway from the westward. And occasions for similar savings will in all probability, nay, will undoubtedly, present themselves again and again, for it would be a fatal mistake to regard the great irrigation works in process of construction in Orissa as safeguards adequate of themselves to secure that province against recurrence of the horrors of 1866. Both there and elsewhere, irrigation, for reasons which will be more particularly adverted to in our next chapter, far from rendering famine impossible, is calculated to aggravate its intensity whenever permitting it to occur, whereas in provinces easily accessible by railway from the rest of the peninsula, the worst evils of drought may, as recent experience has conclusively shown, be successfully obviated. India is a country of such vast extent, and comprises regions so various as to soil, climate, and vicissitudes of weather, that dearth in any quarter is sure to be counterbalanced by extraordinary abundance in others. When the rice crops fail in Bengal, the corn harvests in all probability will be exceptionally heavy in the North-West and the Punjab, and *vice versâ*; or if deficiency of food be general throughout Northern India, then probably there will be redundance in the Deccan or in the farther south, where, in turn, seasons of extreme scarcity will probably correspond with unusually productive seasons in the north; while, in Burmah and the Tenasserim Provinces, moreover, there are granaries generally full to overflowing to be drawn upon in extreme emergencies for the relief of the other side of the Bay of Bengal. Taken as a whole, India never has been, nor, apart from some tremendous visitation against which human foresight would be of no avail, is never likely to be, without sufficient food for all its inhabitants, provided only the means exist of transporting food from districts from which it can be spared to those in which it is lacking. Such means of distribution would be afforded by a complete network of railways, adequately supplemented by common roads; and this consideration will fully justify Government in extending the iron reticulation into many tracts in which such costly undertakings might otherwise be indefensible, and, among the rest, into Chutteesgurh and Orissa.

According to present appearances, however, the claims of these provinces and also of Dharwar, are likely to be postponed for the sake of a region which might better afford to wait for a railway. Among Anglo-Indian territories there is not one that has of late been more rapidly progressive, or is of fairer promise for the future than British Burmah, but neither is there one which is as yet more backward in regard to development of natural resources. Its population, export and import trade, and fiscal revenue have doubled within twelve years, but although on its soil of exuberant fertility enormous quantities of rice are, and almost anything might be, grown, the principal growth is for the present dense jungle, by which half the surface is covered. Nor is this to be wondered at, for of those public works in whose absence no extensive clearance or other important agricultural advances are easily possible, there are scarcely any. With jails, barracks, and other official edifices, Burmah is adequately provided; but of roads there are, or at least were a year or two ago, literally but two: one, 215 miles in length, bisecting the province from Rangoon northward through Prome to Meaday; the other, a branch 35 miles long, from the Prome road to Pegu. The step-motherlike behaviour on the part of the central Government, which this implies, is the greater grievance because Burmah, after paying all her own governmental expenses, contributes a surplus revenue to the imperial exchequer; and the local authorities justly lay stress on this aggravating circumstance in urging local claims. For some time past their loudest demand has been for a railway to be made by laying down rails on the road between Rangoon and Prome. With the usual sanguineness of projectors, they are confident that this line would pay by means of traffic dues alone, as very possibly it before long might; and whether it paid directly or not, it would be sure, by stimulating production, to pay indirectly. To be satisfied of this we have only to listen to what eye-witnesses tell us of the 'marvellous' influence which the common road, proposed to be superseded by the railway, has already had in promoting cultivation. In 1872,

Colonel Oliphant, Chief Engineer in British Burmah, found 'there was hardly a bit of ground to be had within twenty miles of Rangoon, nearly all having been taken up for gardens and plantations, and clearances going on there to a considerable extent,' whereas five years previously, such clearances were 'hardly observable beyond six miles out of Rangoon.' In 1867, while travelling for twenty-four miles between Poungday and Zeegong, along a line of road the earthwork of which was then in the rough, the same officer 'had nothing on either side but tall elephant grass and forest jungle,' but when, early in 1872, he inspected the same section of the then finished road, he observed 'very large areas of paddy cultivation, as well as extensive clearings in progress.' Of the sections north and south of Thongzai, described by Mr. H. Prince in 1869, as running for sixty miles through a 'howling wilderness,' Colonel Oliphant, writing in January 1874, says, 'The development of rice cultivation in the wilderness since the construction of the road has been marvellous. Throughout its whole length is a succession of either new clearings, or land with evidently the first, second, or third year's crop of paddy. The natives are flocking to the district as settlers, the wilderness has ceased to exist, and in a short time will be almost an unbroken sheet of cultivation.' Speaking generally, Colonel Oliphant pronounces it to be 'universally noticeable that, wherever our road is at all approaching completion, there villages spring up and vegetation commences.'

Such being the efficacy of a well-placed common road in stimulating tillage, the case for an equally well-placed railroad may perhaps be considered complete; nor is there indeed anything stronger to be urged in opposition than that, in Burmah, to begin with a railway might be beginning at the wrong end. In order to exert any sensibly beneficial influence beyond its own immediate vicinity, a railway must be easily accessible from places at a distance either by feeder roads or by feeding water-ways. Now of roads of any sort Burmah has at present only the two trunk lines named above. 'Subsidiary roads leading from one great district mart to another are,' says Mr. Eden, the present Chief Commissioner, 'unknown. In the way of making district roads nothing has ever been done. The country is practically without communication except by water and across the fields for a few months of the year.' Water carriage, again, is practicable only during the rainy season, and where there are no creeks or rivers, carriage is at all times a work of immense difficulty, and magnificent plains away from water communication are in consequence left uncultivated. 'I wish to explain,' said, in 1869, General Fytche, Mr. Eden's predecessor, 'that the only way the land revenues of the province can be developed is through the agency of roads. It is true the country is traversed by river highways and creek feeders, but the latter are limited in their extent, and the cultivation is limited in the same way. It is only where a creek will take produce to market that the production exists. Roads to all points where the creeks are navigable are essential to an extension of cultivation.'

Thus, of subsidiary communications, British Burmah

is pronounced on the highest authority to be almost absolutely destitute ; there are as yet no roads by which produce from any distance could be brought to the railway, neither could the creeks and rivers which might assist in rendering this indispensable service do more than assist, unless supplemented by connecting canals or roads, all of which have yet to be made. Now the district through which the projected railway is intended to run may be loosely described as an inverted triangle, 160 miles in height, and with a base of about 40 miles, separated on the west by a row of low hills from the swampy grounds that border the Irrawaddy, and bounded on the east by a range of loftier heights. Not improbably, the construction of the railway might be speedily followed by the conversion of the greater part of this tract into a continuous rice-field, and this might of itself be a sufficient recommendation if the interests of the immediate neighbourhood were the only ones to be considered. In order, however, that the line should be of any use to the ultramontane territories on the east, which are specially in need of its aid, there would have to be created throughout those districts a network more or less complete of common roads and canals, and good cause may be shown why in order of construction these should take precedence of the railway. Even if the railway were actually in existence it would have to wait for the roads and canals before it could become fully effective, whereas the roads and canals, besides being the best preparation for a railway, would, by enabling produce to be brought from the eastward to the existing Prome and Rangoon road, for ulterior conveyance to the sea, to no small extent answer the same purpose as the railway. In other words, the capital laid out on the roads and canals might at once become fully although indirectly remunerative, whereas, if expended on the railway, it might probably exhibit for some years an annual loss, the amount of which, if saved, might have gone far towards covering the cost of the canals and roads. For these reasons, to begin in Burmah by constructing the isolated railway would, as already said, seem to be beginning at the wrong end. A preferable plan would apparently be to begin by providing something like a system of the simplest and least costly, and therefore most easily extensible, yet at the same time most indispensable means of communication, directing them to such points on the present Rangoon and Prome trunk road as may appear best fitted to become hereafter stations on the proposed railway. Nay, it may be a question whether the rough and ready *modus operandi* might not be advantageously pushed farther still. Mr. Eden remarks that during the fair season much produce might be transported over the plains, provided only the water-courses could be crossed. In constructing the district roads, therefore, it might be well to commence by bridging the creeks and rivers met with on the lines selected, and to leave the intermediate earthwork to be executed subsequently.

And not only need not adoption of the order of operations recommended involve any real loss of time, not only may construction of the proposed railway be deferred until the roads, canals, &c. required as feeders shall have been provided, and yet take place quite as early as it will be possible for the line to be productive of much public advantage: there is yet another way in which the interval may be so employed as to assist in securing the ultimate success of the undertaking. In a country like Burmah, utterly destitute of native coal, and where imported coal must always be extravagantly dear, either some cheaper fuel must be obtainable, or the most perfect of railways can be of little more practical utility than wells without water or steam-engines without steam. This is a truth to which in some extensive divisions of India proper, where the same conditions exist, dearly-bought experience has tardily opened the eyes of the administrative authorities, who are now labouring to make up by spasmodic energy for previous want of foresight. In the Madras territories, 'considerable attention has been paid to forming fuel reserves and plantations. In the Cuddapah and Bellary districts there are five plantations and one reserve; and in North Arcot two reserves, occupying ten square miles. In Salem there are large plantations, including some of *Casuarina*, exhibiting astonishing results in growth, some trees planted in 1866 being found in 1874 to contain 14 cubic feet, or half a ton of fuel each. Plantations also have been formed in Trichinopoly and Bolamputty; and in Tinnevelly, tank beds are utilised in this way.' Doubts are entertained, however, whether these woodlands are 'sufficiently extensive, or whether efficient measures to keep out goats, fires, and trespassers have been made, without which poor results and waste of money may be confidently expected.' In the Punjab, likewise, 'the formation of fuel plantations is being assiduously prosecuted; there are flourishing ones of small area at Jullunder, Umritsur, Phillor, Loodiana, and Delhi; and forty-four miles from Delhi is the great Changa Manga plantation, about twelve miles in extent. This, which is now complete, and regularly laid out with export and inspection roads and quarters for the resident officer in charge, and is worked on a regularly drawn up and systematic working plan,' is expected to yield eventually 600,000 maunds (about 28,600 tons) of wood a year for railway consumption. Still it may be as well that the Punjab Forest officers should think nothing done while aught remains to do. After all, in the entire province the extent of newly-planted land is as yet but 20 square miles, whose earliest year of permanent yield is not, despite the marvellous rapidity of Indian vegetation, expected to arrive before 1882, and whose annual yield of fuel thenceforward is estimated at only 57,000 tons, whereas the average firewood demand for the railways of the Punjab and Sind system is already 40,000 tons a year, and will certainly be at least doubled when that system is complete.[1]

In Burmah, fortunately, vast tracts are still covered with primeval forest—tracts so vast as to be frequently spoken of as 'inexhaustible;' but universal experience teaches how purely metaphorical that expression proves, wherever an unlimited demand for wood is allowed to

[1] See Administration Report on the Forest Department for 1872–73, by B. H. Baden Powell, vol. i. pp. 30 and 33.

supply itself without very stringent supervision. 'Even in Burmah,' says Mr. Baden Powell, 'which a superficial observer deems to be one wide expanse of jungle, the regular demand for fuel for any organised steam service soon makes itself felt. The Irrawaddy steamers have required large supplies, and already several tracts near the river in the Prome district have become denuded, and the fuel I saw stacked consisted of wretched billets of thin saplings; *acacia catechu*, the valuable tree that yields the catechu of commerce, being ruthlessly cut for the purpose.'[1] Thus in Burmah, likewise, it is of the first importance that careful estimates should forthwith be prepared of the quantity of fuel likely to be required for railway purposes, and of the extent of woodland capable, under suitable management, of supplying that quantity perennially, and also that whatever active measures may be shown by the estimates to be expedient, should be adopted without further delay. It is due to the local authorities to add that they are apparently fully aware of this necessity, and that they intend to set apart, at intervals of ten miles along the Rangoon and Prome railway, reserves of an aggregate area of probably 100 square miles; and it is only by perseverance in this prudent course that repetition in Burmah of the serious difficulties already experienced elsewhere can be effectually guarded against. The procrastination which may defer the construction of Burmese railways until full security shall have been taken for their being uninterruptedly supplied

[1] See Administration Report on the Forest Department, for 1872–73, by B. H. Baden Powell, vol. i. p. 28.

with the first essential of successful railway working, will certainly not deserve to be stigmatised as a thief of time.[1]

In connexion with the railway fuel question, as affecting India generally, it may not be out of place to advert to two other possible substitutes for ordinary crude coal. Although neither in the southernmost portions of the peninsula, nor yet in the north-west, nor indeed anywhere north of the Ganges, excepting in Assam and some districts immediately adjoining, have any coal strata yet been discovered, extensive beds of the mineral exist in the territories enclosed between the Ganges and the Godavery. In the Damoodah Valley, at a distance of about 120 miles from Calcutta, commences a series of carboniferous tracts, 1,500 square miles in extent, over one-half at least of which area workable seams, varying in thickness from 4½ to 35 ft., occur at depths of not more than 1,000 ft. below the surface. The most important of these tracts is that of Raneegunge, the available coal of which has been roughly estimated by Dr. Oldham at 14,000,000,000 tons, and from which a year's yield was, in 1868, nearly half a million of tons, and has probably become twice as much since, as mining is now going on at forty-four different spots. Another, the Kurhurbaree field, which belongs to, and is worked by, the East Indian Railway Company, covers an area of

[1] Since these passages were written, the construction of the Rangoon and Prome Railway has been formerly authorised, and has made some progress. The remarks in the text have, however, been left standing, as being, many of them, of general application.

eighteen square miles, and is supposed to be capable of yielding 250,000 tons annually for 800 years. In the Nerbudda Valley and north of the Sutpara Hills, is another group of coal fields, and among them one, at Mopani, with a seam of an average thickness of 25 ft. is held on lease by the Nerbudda Coal and Iron Company; and a third group lies on the edge of the great sandstone tract which occupies the valley of the Godavery and its tributaries, the Wurda and Pranhita, from the neighbourhood of Nagpore to that of Ellore. Here, in the Chanda district, is a seam from 50 to 70 ft. thick, stretching over a considerable area; and at and round Wurrora, on the Wurdah, are other beds estimated to contain 10,000,000 tons. Again in Belaspore, and the country west of Chota Nagpore, there are beds of coal, some of them of great thickness; and others are known to exist in South Rewah, in the valley of the Upper Soane and on the Brahminy River.[1] Thus in regard to abundance of supply the accounts are not unpromising; as regards quality the evidence is less satisfactory. In comparison with English coal, Indian contains on an average 52 per cent. of fixed carbon instead of 68, and leaves after combustion from 10 to 30 per cent. of ash instead of 2·7; and bulk for bulk is capable of doing only from one-third to two-thirds of the work performed by English coal. Another defect is its excessive lamination and proportionate friability which, in the case of the

[1] See pages 101–2 of Mr. Clement Markham's Report on the Moral and Material Condition of India during the year 1872—quite a model Report of its kind.

produce of the Wurrora collieries is so great, that Mr. Ness, a mining engineer of large English experience, in charge there, expects the proportion of slack to lump raised to the surface to be as one to three. He is sanguine, however, that the slack, which must otherwise be a worse than useless encumbrance, may be rendered of at least equal economic value with the natural 'lump,' by being formed into artificial blocks; and he speaks with approval of a process for the purpose invented and patented by Mr. Frederick Danvers, of the Indian Office. This, the particulars of which are set forth in detail in Mr. Danvers' published work on 'Coal Economy,' consists in mixing with the coal, after the latter has been minutely disintegrated and cleansed from shale and pyrites by washing, carefully calculated quantities of fatty pitch, farinaceous mucilage, quick-lime and tar, and passing the mixture duly heated into a press, there to be divided into blocks of any shape or size desired; the result arrived at being a substance highly calorific, easily portable, tenacious enough to bear a good deal of knocking about, and waterproof. Mr. Ness reports very favourably of a few hundredweights of fuel which he has himself manufactured at Wurrora in accordance with this method, and, if the inference which he is disposed to draw from these trials be fully borne out by further experiments, Mr. Danvers will have deserved well of the State, and will, it is to be hoped, be rewarded for the time and thought devoted by him to the elaboration of his process, by seeing it generally adopted in Indian collieries.

Another possible substitute for coal is condensed peat,

which, Colonel Romaine Wragge maintains, may be manufactured in large quantities from extensive deposits of the raw material existing on the slopes of the Neilgherry Hills and elsewhere in the Madras Presidency. Colonel Wragge's suggestions have been somewhat summarily pooh-poohed in the belief, arrived at apparently without much examination, that there is but little peat in the Madras territories, and that what there is, is either of little value, or is not in excess of the local demand. Be this as it may, however, it is very unlikely that in some of the numerous hilly tracts of other parts of India, peat should not be comparatively abundant, and if so, it seems a pity that its ability to furnish a fuel suitable for railway use should not be put to the test. As a matter of fact, condensed peat is in actual use as fuel on some of the railways of Continental Europe, where it is found to answer well.

By the contracts between the Indian Government and the several Railway Companies guaranteed by it, power is in every instance reserved—on the one hand to the Government, of purchasing, at specified periods, generally after intervals of twenty-five years, the railway concerned, paying for it the average market value during the three years immediately preceding of the capital stock of the company—on the other hand to the company of, at any time during the currency of its lease, surrendering the railway to Government, receiving in exchange the full amount of capital that may, with the sanction of Government, have been laid out upon it. Some of the dates at which Government's right of compulsory purchase may be exercised are now near at hand, and the expediency of its being exercised accordingly has of late been somewhat warmly debated. On both sides of the question, regarded as a general one, a good deal may be said, but much more for purchase than against it. The strongest, if not the only really valid, argument of general application in favour of non-purchase, and of leaving the companies in possession of their railways as long as they may be willing to retain them, Government proprietorship being meanwhile restricted to the lines which Government has itself constructed, is the healthy emulation which might be expected to arise between State agency and company's agency when operating in close juxtaposition and almost within sight and hearing of each other. Both agencies would then be, as it were, constantly on trial, constantly undergoing a competitive examination before a public very exacting and hypercritical, prone to invidious comparison, and exceedingly intolerant of any shortcomings calculated to impair its own convenience. In presence of such a board of examiners, both agencies would be ever aiming at an ever-rising standard of combined economy and efficiency, would show themselves studious to avoid waste, eager to adopt improvements, solicitous to attract customers by continual offers of additional accommodation; would, in short, present a spectacle of commercial competition so conducive to the general good that it might go far towards conquering the prejudices of my excellent friend Louis Blanc, and reconciling even him to that form of contentiousness.

This is a consideration of no small weight, but it is

more than counterbalanced by others, whereof one is of itself of altogether overwhelming preponderance. In the engagements between the Government and the Railway Companies there are certain peculiarities, in virtue of which Government, by availing itself of the first opportunities of purchase, may acquire most of the railways without paying one farthing for them—without, that is, paying one farthing more than it must have paid whether it had purchased or not. Here, truly, is a startling paradox, but there will be no difficulty in showing that it is simply a paradox—that it involves no particle of absurdity, but is simple and unqualified truth.

The peculiarities alluded to are not indeed equally applicable in all cases, and they are unluckily least applicable in the case of the particular railway which will soonest become purchaseable, and which, moreover, by reason of its magnitude, will, if procurable on favourable terms, be a specially desirable subject of purchase. The following are the earliest dates at which the several railways may, according to contract, be compulsorily purchased:—

East Indian Main Line . . .	February 15, 1879.
„ Jubbulpore Line . .	April 21, 1883.
Eastern Bengal	July 30, 1883.
Sind, Punjab, and Delhi . . .	January 1, 1885.
Oude and Rohilcund . . .	August 2, 1887.
South Indian	March 1, 1890.
Great Indian Peninsula . . .	August 17, 1899.
Bombay, Baroda, and Central India .	May 1, 1905.
Madras	April 1, 1907.

From this table it appears that of the two portions, the

main and Jubbulpore lines, of which the East Indian Railway is composed, the company may, four years hence, be required to sell the first and larger portion. They may, if they choose, retain the Jubbulpore line for another four years, but it is very unlikely that they will so choose, and will not rather, if constrained to part with one of the undertakings, prefer to part with both. In that case the purchase to which the Government will stand committed will be that of the company's entire property, the price to be paid for which will be the average market value during the three years immediately preceding, of the company's capital stock. This market value it will not be safe to reckon at less than 15 per cent. above par, so that, the amount of capital stock being in round numbers thirty millions sterling, the amount payable by Government will be 34,500,000*l.* In the present state of its credit the Indian Government might be able to borrow a few millions, perhaps as many as seven or eight, at 4 per cent., but for 34½ millions it would certainly have to submit to a much higher rate, to 6 or 7 per cent. or more; and to borrow at such a rate for purchase of a railway earning at the rate of only 6 per cent. on 30 millions, and therefore of only a trifle above 5 per cent. on the supposed purchase money, would obviously be the reverse of a promising speculation. If then it were obligatory to pay for the line at once in a lump sum, the purchase of the East Indian railway could scarcely commend itself to a prudent financier.

It fortunately happens, however, that the contracts with this and most of the railway companies give to the

Government the option of, instead of paying the whole purchase money down at once, commuting it for an equivalent annuity for 75 years, 'calculated at a rate of interest to be determined by the average rate of interest during the two preceding years received in London on public obligations' of the Indian Government. Now as there are no longer any such public obligations on which other rates than 4 and 5 per cent. are received, the average rate must be something between 4 and 5 per cent. Just now it is 4·441, or a trifle less than 4*l.* 9*s.*, below which figure it may not improbably fall a little, but above which it is pretty certain not to rise within the next four years. 4*l.* 9*s.*, therefore, may be taken as the highest rate at which the annuity can have to be calculated, and, at that rate, the annuity for 75 years equivalent to 34½ millions is in round numbers 1,600,000*l.* But the net earnings of the East Indian Railway are at present about 6 per cent. on its capital stock of 30 millions, and for our present purpose may be confidently regarded as sure to continue at not less than that percentage, for it is only on that supposition that the stock has been taken at so high a premium as 15, and the amount required for its redemption at 34½ millions. But 6 per cent. on 30 millions is 1,800,000*l.*, out of which amount of annual net earnings, therefore, Government will, throughout the whole 75 years, be able to take 1,600,000*l.* a year for the payment of the annuity, without once putting its hand into its own pocket except to deposit therein an annual surplus of 200,000*l.*

It thus appears that purchase of the East Indian, the least manageable of all the railways, would in all probability cost the Government, not simply nothing, but considerably less than nothing: would take nothing out of the pockets of the purchaser, but on the contrary would annually divert into them considerable sums which would otherwise have become divisible amongst the sellers. Much the same thing would happen in the case of the Eastern Bengal, whose turn for purchase will come next, viz. in July 1883, about eight years hence. The net earnings of this line are actually about 5 per cent. on its capital stock, and, according to present appearances, are not likely either to rise materially above or to sink sensibly below that percentage during the next eight years. During the same period, therefore, the market value of the capital stock may likewise be expected to remain much the same as at present, viz. at 12 per cent. above par, at which price, the total stock, being in round numbers 3,200,000*l.*, will be worth nearly 3,600,000*l.* Should the Government desire to pay this amount in the form of an annuity it will be able, in 1883, to do so on terms a good deal easier for itself than those which had been incumbent upon it in a corresponding transaction with the East Indian Railway a few years earlier. For it will in 1880 have acquired the right, which it will surely not have failed to exercise, of either paying off its 5 per cent. stock, or of reducing the interest thereon to 4 per cent. thereby causing 4 per cent. to be the 'average rate of interest during the two years' preceding 1883, 'received in London upon public obligations of the Indian Government,' and consequently rendering the same rate the rate of interest to be used in calculating the annuity. Now at 4 per cent. the annuity for 75 years equivalent to 3,600,000*l.* is one of 152,000*l.*; but, although bound to pay this for 75 years, Government will, according to the hypothesis, be receiving in the shape of net railway earnings, at least 5 per cent. on 3,200,000*l.*—will be receiving, that is, at least 160,000*l.* a year, out of which, after deduction of the annuity, there will accrue to Government a net annual surplus of nearly 18,000*l.*

Besides, although in dealing with the Eastern Bengal Railway Company, the mode of payment most advantageous to Government would be that of an annuity, Government need not, unless it choose, adopt that course, but may, if it prefer, pay off the entire purchase money at once. For in the present and reasonably prospective state of its credit, it would have no difficulty in borrowing so moderate an amount as 3,600,000*l.* at 4 per cent., paying, therefore, for its use no more than 144,000*l.* yearly, which, if deducted from 160,000*l.* of annual net earnings, would leave a balance of 16,000*l.* This, if suffered to accumulate at 4 per cent. compound interest, would in 59 years become 3,600,000*l.* the amount needed to pay back the principal borrowed, and, after the 59th year until the 75th, it would be so much annually added to the Government income. Here again, then, whichever mode be adopted, the sellers themselves will, as in the case of the East Indian Railway, not merely provide the purchase money annually, but will make besides a handsome present to the purchaser.

None of the other railways are likely to become the subjects of equally brilliant operations: none of them hold out prospects of similar or similarly early profit:

still, so far as mere purchaseability for nothing goes, there is perfect certainty of that condition applying to all but three of them. Take, for example, the Sind, Punjab, and Delhi line, the least promising of any, and also the third in succession to become compulsorily purchaseable. This line belongs to a company with a capital stock of 10½ millions sterling, on which the net profits have never yet, except in one season of very peculiar circumstances, exceeded 1½ per cent. or three-tenths of the guaranteed interest. Some improvement may doubtless be looked for, when by interposition of the link still missing between Moultan and Kotree, continuous railway communication shall have been established between Delhi and Lahore, and thence to Kurrachee; but the improvement is sure to be slow, and cannot apparently ever be sufficient to confer complete financial success on a railway trammelled with all the costly encumbrances of a 5 ft. 6 in. gauge, yet running for great part of its course through a country well named 'Young Egypt,' on account of the vast breadths of arid waste that hem in its two slender strips of cultivated land. We shall be erring, therefore, if at all, only on the side of prudence by assuming that the remunerativeness of the line will continue much the same as at present for some two or three generations, and by taking the maximum of its prospective net earnings at 2 per cent. on its cost. Still, thanks to the Government guarantee, the stock even of the Sind, Delhi, and Punjab Railway is actually and will no doubt continue to be at a considerable premium, and may very likely be in 1885 as much as 12 per cent. above par: on which supposition the market value of a total of 10½ millions sterling will be 11,760,000*l.* This is too large an amount to be borrowed on moderate terms, and will therefore have to be commuted into an annuity. But, as before explained, the rate to be used in calculating the annuity will in 1885 be 4 per cent., at which rate the annuity for 75 years, equivalent to 11,760,000*l.*, is one of 496,600*l.* Towards payment of this the Government will, according to the hypothesis, obtain from railway earnings only 210,000*l.* at most, and will therefore be annually 286,600*l.* out of pocket. But if it had neglected to purchase, it would have had to make up the difference between the 2 per cent. on 10½ millions, or 210,000*l.* of net earnings, and the 5 per cent., or 525,000*l.*, of guaranteed interest; it would, that is, have had to pay to the railway company 315,000*l.* a year. The difference between the two operations is this, that in the latter case the Government would make a payment of 315,000*l.* a year for 75 years, or of about 24 millions in all, without obtaining any return, whereas in the former case it would, by 75 payments of 286,000*l.* each, or less than 22 millions in all, become absolute proprietor of the railway.

The circumstances of the remaining railways do not need to be examined with the same minuteness. From what has been said of the East Indian, the Eastern Bengal, and the Sind, Punjab, and Delhi, it may be inferred in regard also to the South Indian and to the Oude and Rohilcund, that, if purchased at the earliest dates permitted by contract, these too may, each of them, become the property of Government without money and without price, even though their respective net earnings continue for 75 years thereafter to be below the amount of interest which Government has conditionally guaranteed: while in the event of net earnings equalling or exceeding the guaranteed interest, Government will not simply get the lines for nothing, but will be saved a great deal of money which, if it had neglected to purchase, it would have been obliged to pay. It will not indeed be at liberty to effect the purchase by means of annuities, the clause conveying option to that effect having been omitted from the contracts with the South Indian and Oude and Rohilcund Railway Companies. The amount of purchase money to be raised is not, however, in either case very large—not more than 4 millions sterling for the South Indian, nor than 6 millions for the Oude and Rohilcund; and moreover, if it should for any reason be temporarily impossible to raise the required amounts at moderate rates, the Government will then, by virtue of a special clause substituted, in the contracts with the South Indian and Oude and Rohilcund Companies, for the annuity clause, be at liberty, instead of paying cash, to transfer to the company concerned such an amount of 5 per cent. Indian stock as would at par be equal to the cash due, reserving to itself the right of redeeming the stock at par at any subsequent time. Government will thus be able to bide its time, and defer completion of purchase until cash for the purpose shall again become obtainable on moderate terms.

In favour of the general policy here advocated, another argument may be urged of even greater cogency than any yet adduced. The date is not very remote at which, if Government have until then neglected to exercise its power of compulsory purchase, it will be compelled to purchase, whether it will or not. By certain clauses, placed in curious juxtaposition in each of the contracts, it is provided that, if the building lease under which the railway has been constructed be suffered to run to the end of its term (usually of 100 years), the railway and all its appurtenances shall *ipso facto* become the property of Government, without payment of any kind in return; whereas if the company in the 99th or other penultimate year take the precaution of giving notice to that effect, it may at the close of the final year surrender the railway to Government, which will then be bound to reimburse the company whatever amount of capital may, with its consent, have been expended on the railway. Of course, any company that may be allowed the chance, will take care to exercise this latter option, and the consequence will be that Government, which, by previously observing certain prescribed forms of purchase, might have obtained the railway for less than nothing, will then have to pay such sums as the following—for the East Indian, 30,000,000*l.*; for the Eastern Bengal, 3,200,000*l.*; and for the Sind, Punjab, and Delhi, 10,500,000*l.*, and the last of these amounts, too, after having irrecoverably paid to the Sind, Punjab, and Delhi Company, as the difference between net earnings and guaranteed interest for 75 years, no less than 23,625,000*l.*, the whole of which it might, by purchasing in the 25th year, have got back long before the 100th. The choice as yet open to Government being thus not between purchase and non-purchase, but between purchase for nothing and purchase at an enormous outlay, the choice that will be made cannot be doubtful. Neglect of so splendid an opportunity of making all the railways of a country national property on terms which would allow of the use of the railways being afforded to the public at rates and fares just sufficient to cover the expenses of maintenance and working, would be a breach of trust, of which no Government, and least of all the Anglo-Indian Government, can be supposed capable.

There are, however, three railways, the Great Indian Peninsula, the Bombay and Baroda, and the Madras, which stand in a different category from the rest, Government's right of purchasing them in the 25th year of the lease having been not long ago surrendered, with an unfortunate short-sightedness which, as the present writer acknowledges that he fully shared it at the time, he may perhaps with the less scruple presume to condemn now. The earliest date at which Government will now be entitled to purchase any of these three is the 50th year, when the annuity substitutable for the purchase money must, according to contract, be one for 50 years, and doubtless therefore much too large to be paid out of annual net earnings. The net earnings, however, of the Great Indian Peninsula and of the Bombay and Baroda are already close upon 5 per cent. and are not unlikely before long to bear continuously much about that proportion to capital, thereby relieving Government from further claims on account of guaranteed interest. On this supposition it may be the best plan for Government to wait until these two railways are, in the 100th year of their respective leases, spontaneously surrendered, when the price to be paid for them will be, not the market value of the capital stock, but only the actual cost of the railway—an amount less than that of the market value by not less probably than 12 per cent. Not so, however, with regard to the Madras line, whose net receipts exhibit little tendency to rise above their present low level of 3 per cent. on the capital. In this instance, Government may gain considerably by purchasing in the 50th year, as otherwise it may have to go on for other fifty years paying away immense sums under the name of guaranteed interest, which, instead of being fruitlessly so expended, might just as easily have been applied, as far as they would go, towards purchase of the railway. Arithmetically stated, the case will stand thus: capital stock being taken at 10½ millions, and its market value at 12 premium, or 11,760,000*l.*, annual net earnings at 3 per cent. on 10½ millions, or 315,000*l.*, and the difference between net earnings and guaranteed interest at 2 per cent. or 210,000*l.*—Government, neglecting to purchase in the 50th year, will have to pay this last amount annually for fifty years, or 10,600,000*l.* altogether, getting nothing whatever in return, and yet at the end of the 100th year will still be obliged to pay 10½ millions for the railway. In other words, its aggregate payments will be 210,000*l.* × 50 = 10,600,000*l.* + 10,500,000*l.* = 21,100,000*l.*; whereas if it had voluntarily purchased in the 50th year instead of waiting to be forced to purchase in the 100th, the aggregate demands upon it would have been only an annuity of 547,000*l.*—210,000*l.* =337,000*l.* × 50 = 16,850,000*l.*, the difference in favour of Government in the latter transaction being 425,000*l.*

To all that has been said a very natural objection no doubt is that it proceeds on the assumption of certain exceedingly fickle conditions remaining long unchanged, and that quite possibly in 1879, 1883, 1885, 1899, 1905, or 1907, the credit of the Indian Government may have deteriorated or the intrinsic value of money have risen. But to this it may be answered, firstly, that the rate of interest to be used in calculating the annuity into which the purchase money of any of the Indian railways may be converted, will not necessarily be at all affected by the state of Government's credit at any precise date, but will be determined by the average rate of interest receivable in London on the obligations of the Indian Government during the two previous years, and this average is almost certain not to exceed 4 per cent.; and, secondly, that in proportion as the value of money in the general market rises, the market value of railway company stock may be expected to fall, so that, if Government be on the one hand compelled to pay higher interest for what money it borrows, it will on the other hand have to borrow less in order to purchase a guaranteed railway. The only disturbing influences which seem to me really capable of invalidating the conclusions arrived at are, first, the sharp practice on the Stock Exchange—technically, I believe, called 'rigging the market'—whereby the average market value of Indian Railway Stock might be factitiously raised in anticipation of purchase by Government; and, secondly, a decrease in the remunerativeness of the railways consequent on their being taken under Government management. The first-mentioned of these dangers I must leave to be discussed by experts, confessing my own utter incompetence to judge of its reality or extent. The second, however, irrespectively of any particular issue depending upon it, deserves to be investigated on general grounds.

The besetting sins of Government agency are manifest, and are these: apathy, prodigality, pedantic pig-headedness. Once upon a time dishonesty might have been added to the list, but among ourselves at least there is no longer room for such reproach; and there is now no body of men more generally imbued with a high sense of duty than English public servants. Their dutifulness must, however, be admitted to be rather of the passive than of the active species, and to be as a rule but little apt to display itself in the form of over-exertion. Both those who are directly engaged in executive work, and those who superintend the performance of the work, are aware that theirs is neither a very exacting nor a nicely discriminating taskmaster. They have no confidence that by extra pains they will improve their position or recommend themselves for promotion, and they too commonly, therefore, content themselves with taking just that modicum of pains which they consider will secure them against dismissal. Their master's dignity, too, seems to them to be above solicitude about petty savings, and also to demand of them in all their movements a slow stateliness of pace, the direct reverse of fussy haste, and an habitual preference for old-fashioned familiar ways, the *antiquas vias* of routine, to any short innovating cuts. Imbued with such notions and giving itself such airs, Government agency often makes but a sorry figure beside self-dependent private enterprise: but in the present instance, the agency to be contrasted with it is private agency in leading strings—a guaranteed private agency from which every particle of either independence or enterprise has been carefully eliminated; and from comparison with this it has no occasion to shrink. For easy a taskmaster as a Government may be, an Indian railway company is yet easier, since unless it have, which only one or two of the companies have, a tolerably near prospect of earning more than the guaranteed interest, it lacks the most potent motive for vigilance or strictness of control. However badly affairs be conducted and however insignificant the surplus of receipts over working expenses, directors and shareholders are equally sure of their 5 per cent.: equally without hope of more or danger of less. Besides, however anxious to exercise efficient supervision, Boards of Direction, sitting in London, can know little more of what their agents are doing on the other side of the globe than the agents think proper to tell them. They have no alternative but to accept almost without reserve the representations of their chief functionaries, who, for anything the so-called directors can do to prevent them, are pretty much at liberty to follow the leading of their own sweet will, for decency and consistency's sake allowing to their subordinates latitude similar to that assumed by themselves. But the Indian

Government, being on the spot, and having all its railway operations immediately under its own observation, would not have to take for granted whatever it was told by the railway staff, but would be able to look into matters with its own eyes and to pounce down at once on sluggishness or unskilfulness or waste or malversation. Shortcomings too of every description, which might remain for ever unsuspected by a distant Board, would, even without being looked for, force themselves on the attention of the local Government. For the members of the latter, individually and collectively, personally and by proxy, in their private and in their official capacity, constitute a portion of the Indian community which, more almost than any other, has frequent occasion to avail itself of railway communication. They could scarcely therefore fail to become aware if railway operations for which they were ultimately responsible were not proceeding satisfactorily, and they have too direct an interest in proper procedure not to take pains to discover which of their employees were in fault, and to make examples of the chief delinquents for the encouragement of the others. Not that such examples would be so likely to be needed as under the present system. For whereas the servants of remote railway companies have little, if any, personal interest in the success of the undertakings in which they are engaged, Government servants would, to say nothing of higher motives, feel that their official advancement depended on their performance of their official duties; and, when good service was insisted upon by their employers as a condition of promotion, would, for their own sakes, do their best to render what was required. Moreover, there would be the past experience and example of the companies to assist in showing what errors and dangers were to be avoided, while at the same time both Government and its servants would feel bound, in justification of their having superseded the railway companies, to do better than the companies had done. The officers employed by Government would thus be on their mettle, and here it is incumbent on me to remark, in qualification of a previous somewhat disparaging observation, that though of public servants as a class, owing to the depressing atmosphere that commonly surrounds them, apathy be notoriously a besetting sin, still there is no such self-devotion as that of exceptional members of the class, while even its average members require little to stimulate them to extraordinary exertion. In fact, it is to servants of the public alone, to the exclusion of those of all other employers, that public zeal and public spirit come at all naturally; while among such of them as are good for anything, these qualities are always ready to show themselves as soon as called for. Those employees are not worth their salt who do not take a disinterested pride in any work of theirs which they perceive to conduce to a great public end, and who, because it so conduces, will not apply themselves to it with a will, impossible for those the immediate object of whose labour is to make one or more other persons rich. But for those who are worth so much, when they are pitted against the servants of private employers, individual or corporate, with equal encouragement to do their best, there need be no doubt of their doing at least equally well. And great national undertakings like national State railways are specially calculated to elicit disinterested zeal. Whenever, then, the guaranteed railways of India may be brought under State management, there need be no fear that, in a land proverbially so fertile in heroes of every variety, there will be any lack of Rowland Hills or Frank Ives Scudamores to prevent their remunerativeness from falling below its present level.

Merely to do as well as the guaranteed companies are doing would, however, be no very creditable achievement, and Government in its railway management will, it is to be hoped, aim at a much higher standard—the more surely to attain which it may not be superfluous to reinforce public spirit by enlisting self-interest on the same side. One means thereto might be to have recourse to that form of the co-operative principle which makes labour's remuneration partly dependent on its productiveness, by assigning to it, in addition to salary or wages, a share in any profits in excess of a specified amount. In illustration of this expedient I shall perhaps be pardoned for extracting the following passage from a former work of my own :—

'There is no doubt that workpeople in general could, if they pleased, do more and better work than they usually do. One naturally works more with a will when working for one's-self than for a master, and when doing piece-work than when paid by time. Most men too are willing to work harder for the sake of proportionately better pay.

If they were not, there would not be so much readiness on the part of all workers, except trades unionists, to take piece-work. Neither would employers be so ready to give it them, unless experience had shown that when earnings are made dependent on the work done, the work done may generally be depended upon for being of not less value than the earnings. Now all co-operative labour partakes largely of the character of piece-work. Unless a certain quantity of work of not less than a certain quality be done, the men get nothing but bare wages, while for every addition to the quantity, and every improvement in the quality, they are assured of some bonus in addition. They are thus directly interested in being diligent and careful. They have a similar assurance with respect to every saving of material they effect, and they are thus interested in being economical likewise, which in piece-work they are not. What is still more to the purpose is that every individual is even more interested in seeing that the industrial virtues are practised by his companions, than in practising them himself. The superintending efficacy of the master's eye is everywhere proverbial. There is nothing like it for preventing hands from slurring over toilsome or tedious operations. But the master's eye cannot be everywhere, and as business is ordinarily conducted, where it is wanting, there is nothing to supply its place. But when capital takes labour into partnership, every labourer in becoming a partner becomes also a partaker in a master's motives for vigilance. The interest which any one such petty partner can have in watching over the prosperity of the common undertaking is not indeed to be compared with the solicitude of a single employer for a concern exclusively his own, but the conjunction of many units produces an aggregate of superintending vigilance more efficacious than that of any single master. Each one knows that the amount divisible between his companions and himself depends on the manner in which he and they do their work; and even though this do not induce him to do his best himself, it will at least make him anxious that the others should do theirs. Thus every one is watched by every one else. Every one has upon him not one, but perhaps hundreds of pairs of eyes, and every eye the eye of a master. The consequence is well shown in the business of Messrs Briggs' (owners of collieries near Normanton, in Yorkshire), 'For one thing, the expense of overlookers is sensibly diminished. The miners overlook one another of their own accord without asking to be paid for it; rating those sharply who are not working properly, and likewise those who are guilty of wastefulness. According to evidence given by one of themselves, it is quite a common thing now for a man, in passing through the yard, if he meet with a bolt or a large nail, to pick it up, and say, "This is so much bonus saved," and the same with the men in the pits. They will sometimes get out a prop rather difficult to remove, and which might under other circumstances have been left, and then will turn over the expression of "so much saved towards bonus."'[1]

[1] On Labour, 2nd edition, p. 391–2.

It is thus abundantly clear that labour may, by the prospect of increased reward, be stimulated to increased productiveness sufficient to furnish wherewithal, not only to pay the increased reward, but also to reward employers for their sagacious liberality in trying the experiment. It will not, then, I trust be deemed to be through mere fondness for a hobby of my own that I presume to urge the Indian Government to take into 'industrial partnership,' all the employees, from the highest to the lowest, who may be engaged in working any of its railways. Neither need it defer trying this plan until it shall by purchase have acquired the position now occupied by some one of the guaranteed companies. It may at once begin with those other railways which it is itself constructing, and one of which has already been partially opened for traffic. With every engineer of every grade, from 'first-class chief,' to apprentice, and every supervisor and overseer intent for his own sake in maintaining the line and its appurtenances in the best possible order at the least possible expense, with locomotive superintendents watching with similar vigilance over the rolling stock, and traffic managers ever on the look out for customers, and even stokers and firemen perceiving that every pound of coal or ounce of oil wasted was so much diverted from a bonus fund in which they were entitled to participate, even railways designed rather with political and military views than for commercial purposes, even those traversing so meagre a soil as that of Rajpootana, may not impossibly turn out to be commercially profitable. True the edifying spectacle in that case presented might cause the co-operative principle to be adopted on the guaranteed lines also, and, by rendering these more financially successful, raise proportionately the market value of their capital stock; but although the Government would in consequence have eventually to pay a good deal more for the guaranteed railways, it could console itself by the reflection that in return for more money it would acquire more money's worth.

A great collateral advantage which will result from acquisition by the State of all Indian railways is the increased facility which will thereby be afforded for establishment of complete uniformity of gauge. All the guaranteed lines, with the single exception of the South Indian, have at present a gauge of 5 ft. 6 in.; with two insignificant exceptions, of all those constructed by Government, the gauge is of one metre, or 3 ft. 3 in., so that, at almost every point at which guaranteed and State lines touch, break of gauge ensues. Now, although the evils of break of gauge have often in the heat of controversy been ludicrously exaggerated, they are very far indeed from imaginary. Although at the worst they plainly cannot be worse than those incidental to the first stowage in a railway train of passengers or goods brought in cabs or carts to the railway station, and cannot therefore deserve to be stigmatised as 'infinite,' 'incalculable,' or 'of an amount not to be represented by figures,' they are nevertheless always quite bad enough to make themselves distinctly felt from the beginning, and they become more and more serious in proportion as traffic increases. It may be that for a considerable time to come the traffic of the Indian metre gauge lines will be principally local; yet even now, to a passenger taking his ticket at Meerut for Jeypore, it must be nearly as great a bore to have to change carriages at Delhi, as it is for a Londoner, who has occasion to go from Waterloo to Norbiton by the 3 P.M. train, to be obliged to get out at Wimbledon; and what is merely a bore to a stray civilian or two is magnified into a nuisance when a considerable body of troops are concerned, or when some truck loads of heavy merchandise, Sambhur Lake salt or the like, have to be transferred from gauge to gauge. Besides, Indian railways of both descriptions will greatly disappoint expectation, if the development of industrial resources promoted by them do not eventually superadd to local traffic such an amount of through traffic as will render the trouble, delay, and expense of break of gauge almost intolerable. But by that time too, not simply the perfect sufficiency for all practical purposes of the metre gauge, but also its great economical superiority over its rival, will doubtless have been demonstrated by experience too conclusively to allow of the idea of abandoning that gauge to be entertained for a moment. The obvious alternative therefore to widening, at an average cost of at least 1,000*l.* a mile, the 10,000 miles of narrow gauge railway expected to be at no distant period required, will be to narrow, at a cost of at most 500*l.* a mile, the 5,000 miles of existing broad gauge lines; and this course the Government, when relieved from the necessity of humouring the prejudices of proprietary companies, will be at liberty gradually to adopt. On one broad gauge line after another it will be able to take up the rails, and to relay them metre gauge, removing at the same time the no longer suitable broad gauge rolling stock to other lines still using it. When this transformation has been completed, one of the great mistakes of Lord Dalhousie's original arrangements will have been corrected; waste of power and carriage space will have been reduced to a minimum, and the expense of maintaining railway communication being thus most materially diminished, a proportionate reduction will become practicable in the charges made for railway accommodation. The manifold advantages resulting from this mode of establishing universal uniformity of gauge will be great everywhere, but—as the obligations of official loyalty need not, I trust, prevent my adding—they will nowhere else be so great as in the Punjab and in the other territories watered by the Indus and its affluents. And this, not simply because the scanty traffic of those territories is peculiarly unable to support an extravagantly costly system of transport, but also and far more, because the adoption there of the metre gauge will admit of certain highly desirable railway extensions, the cost of which would otherwise be utterly prohibitory. The purposes for which the Punjab railways have been designed are in only a very minor degree commercial: they are mainly political and military, and have indeed avowed reference to the possibility of an invasion from a basis of operations westward of Afghanistan. In view of such a contingency, our only wise policy is obviously the generous one of making common cause with Afghanistan, and endeavouring to enlist her on our side, not as a protected and coerced dependent, but as an independent ally whose strength it is our interest by all legitimate means to foster and reinforce. If the Afghans can be persuaded that such is sincerely our policy, they will, in the supposed contingency, far from opposing, cordially welcome the entry into and passage through their country of British troops; and the aid afforded to such movements by railways running westwardly from Peshawur, Mooltan, and Sukkur towards Cabool, Candahar, Quetta and Khelat, may on occasion become invaluable. On this point I need not perhaps apologise for extracting the following very apposite remarks from a Minute by the Marquis of Salisbury. 'That we shall never,' says his Lordship, in reference to the defence of India against invasion from the westward, 'engage in any but a defensive war is almost certain; but it by no means follows that our defensive war will consist only of defensive operations. It is always a possibility that an advance into Khelat or beyond it may be a necessary portion of our strategy. If so, regiments, horses, and material will require to be passed on as rapidly as railways can carry them.'[1] But railways in the directions specified, traversing as they would, little else than an alternation of rocky ridge and sandy waste, and certain therefore to be at first and long to continue almost utterly unremunerative, cannot possibly be permitted to imitate the type of those broad Indian lines whose cost of construction has averaged 17,000*l.* a mile. They must, if made at all, needs be made of a comparatively inexpensive narrow gauge. Yet

[1] Parliamentary Paper, No. 372 of 1874.

narrow gauge lines branching off westwardly from a broad gauge in the Indus Valley would commence with breaks of gauge at specially inconvenient places, and would thus lose at the very outset much of the military utility which had been the great object of their construction. The previous conversion to narrow gauge of the existing Punjab railways is, therefore, an indispensable condition of the westwardly extensions alluded to; and this is a consideration which I respectfully submit has not hitherto been taken sufficiently into account.

CHAPTER III.

IRRIGATION.

Ἄριστον μὲν ὕδωρ: There is nothing like water: so may not inappropriately commence a chapter on Indian Irrigation, a subject as well worthy as most to be treated Pindarically. 'Three things there are,' according to Agur, son of Jakeh, 'that are never satisfied; yea, four never say "it is enough."' For one of the four the curious enquirer may be referred to the thirtieth chapter of Proverbs; the other three are the grave, fire, and 'the earth that is not filled with water.' Now, of the seven regions into which India has for hygrometric purposes been divided by Dr. Brandis,[1] there are but two that have their fill of water from natural sources—the one extending from the mouth of the Irrawaddy, along the east coast of the Bay of Bengal, up the valley of the Brahmaputra, and along the skirts of the Himalayas; the other along the west coast of the Peninsula from the sea-shore to the summits of the Ghauts. A third, indeed, comprising the Deltas of the Mahanuddy and the Ganges, and also the lower part of the Gangetic valley, has a

[1] Markham's Moral and Material Progress, p. 49. Dr. Brandis is at present Inspector-General of Indian Forests.

yearly rainfall of between 60 in. and 75 in.; and in a fourth, made up of the upper valley of the Ganges, Central India, and the east coast of the Madras Presidency, the fall is between 30 and 60 inches; but in the extreme south, between Nassick and Cape Comorin, and also in an extensive stretch of territory adjacent to Delhi and Agra, it is only from 15 to 30 inches, while throughout Sind, and in one-half of the Punjab, it is less than 15 inches.

In the drier regions, too, the rainfall is precarious as well as scanty. Not only do wide expanses of good soil lie permanently untilled and tenantless, but, in the cultivated tracts, a yet more melancholy spectacle is presented when the famishing peasantry have been disappointed of the accustomed discharge from the sky, and fields sown in spring are covered in the autumn with nothing but withered herbage. As for the Punjab and Sind, good part of the former and the whole of the latter would be scarcely habitable without irrigation, which consequently must have been practised there from very remote antiquity, the appliances at first adopted for the purpose and still in most general use, being wells and inundation canals. These latter are artificial cuts or adapted natural watercourses leading off from both sides of the Indus and its affluents, and creating along the river banks narrow strips of luxuriant vegetation. For the most part they are very unskilfully planned and rudely executed, having generally no headworks, and being in fact little better than shallow trenches from 15 to 20 ft. wide, and from 5 or 6 to 60 or 70 miles in length. They are empty during the winter, receiving no water except when the rivers are swollen by the melted snow of the Himalayas, and receiving it then at a level which prevents its being carried very far inland. Still they suffice very tolerably for the limited extent of land within their reach. At midsummer, when they obtain their maximum supply, and when the sky is brass, and but for them the earth would everywhere be like iron, the alternating gardens and cornfields, interspersed with groves of date palms, through which they flow, contrast deliciously with the boundless prospect of scrubby moor and naked sand beyond. Under British management the inundation canals have been materially improved. Some that had almost entirely disappeared, leaving only some faint traces to mark their ancient course, have been restored. Of some the previously tortuous course has been straightened, others have been deepened a foot or more throughout, or have been widened at the head or tail, or have had their tails extended, or additional branches cut from them, or have been furnished with new and larger mouths. One serious defect of all is liability to have their mouths closed, or separated from the source of replenishment, by deposits of silt left there, or by recession of the river, and for remedying these evils comprehensive schemes have been devised which would provide permanent masonry heads at points whence entire series of canals might be permanently supplied. Any such projects, however, would be exceedingly costly, and it may be doubted whether the decision would be in their favour if simple arithmetic were called upon to determine whether continuance of the present rude system, notwithstanding the constant expense and trouble it demands, would not yield more largely remunerative returns.

In the south-eastern quarter of the Madras Presidency, irrigation is but one degree less indispensable than in the Punjab, and has probably been practised from an equally remote date, though the method originally adopted was different, being that of tanks or reservoirs of various sorts and sizes. Into some, when the rivers are in flood, watercourses pour a portion of their contents, to be held in reserve until the approaching season of drought. Others are filled by the rains, or are formed by throwing across the valley of some small stream a dam, behind which a sheet of water is presently formed, often as large as, and sometimes as beautiful as Windermere or Ulleswater. Where the contour of the country permits, several tanks follow each other in a connected series. The first embankment is thrown across a gorge high enough up to retain sufficient water for all the irrigable land lower down, and 'descending terraces are occupied by a succession of reservoirs, the higher feeding the lower from its surplus supply.' Many tanks have been suffered to fall into ruin, but there are said to be still no less than 43,000 in different parts of the Madras Presidency, with 30,000 miles of embankment, and 300,000 separate masonry works.[1] In North Arcot, Madura and Tinnevelly, as shown on the sheets of the Trigonometrical Survey, they dot the land as thickly as the holes in a cullender.

[1] Markham's Moral and Material Progress of India, p. 71.

The same Presidency contains also the most ancient specimen of a class of works of a still more ambitious character, whereby the largest rivers may be rendered subservient to agriculture. Nothing can be more variable than the aspect of Indian rivers at different seasons. In spring and early summer, when swollen by melted snow from the mountains, or by the deluging monsoon rains, the smallest become furious torrents, rising to an extraordinary height wherever confined between high banks, and spreading far and wide over the country on both sides wherever they can find an outlet. After the rains, the largest dwindle into rivulets which are everywhere fordable, and over which in many places a child might step dry footed. The Indus, Ganges, and Brahmaputra, are almost the only exceptions to this rule, and even the Indus, which in July rises to a height of 50 ft. between Attock and Kalabagh, cannot six months later be navigated without difficulty by boats of more than 2 ft. draught. Simultaneously with these variations in the rivers, the land experiences a nearly corresponding alternation of disaster, being now liable to be devastated by overwhelming floods, and presently afterwards to be left panting with thirst for want of the very water which, after laying it waste, has itself run to waste in the sea. The problem for the hydraulic engineer, therefore, is so to regulate the flow of the rivers, and so to arrange the supply of water to the land, as to convert into a constant blessing that of which the excess or the deficiency is an equally fatal curse. For this purpose the ordinary course is to throw across a river, what in Bengal and the North-Western

Provinces is called a bund, and in the Madras territories an annicut—in plain English, a gigantic weir, which arrests the passage of the stream and raises it to a higher level. From the reservoir thus formed, are led off canals, having generally a much higher elevation than the natural river, and from them branch off secondary canals of smaller dimensions which distribute the fertilising element over the lowlands on either side, and the continually diminishing ramifications of which disperse it to every estate, to every village and farm, and almost to every field.

According to tradition, the first to whom the conception of designs so magnificent occurred was a Hindoo Rajah, one Veranum, supposed to have flourished within a century or two of the Christian era—whether before or after is much disputed, and does not greatly matter. Tanjore, the province over which he ruled, cannot be said to have been particularly favoured by nature, for its soil was originally a poor light sand, but it is fortunately intersected by a considerable stream, the Cauvery, which has been turned to such excellent account that the plains adjacent are now unsurpassed in productiveness by the richest Gangetic alluvial deposits. A bird's-eye view of the country would now embrace a minutely ramifying arterial system, from whose main branches innumerable rills run off in every direction, saturating a wide expanse of absorbent soil, from which very little water escapes to dribble into the sea through a few petty outlets. The prospect would be one of an interminable rice-field, diversified by groves of cocoa-nut trees, and occasional patches of maize, millet, indigo, and tobacco. In short, by anticipation of the self-same treatment subsequently applied with such beneficial results to the chief affluents of the Po, Tanjore has been brought into a condition which has obtained for it the name of the Indian Lombardy, though it might perhaps be more chronologically accurate to give to Lombardy the name of the Italian Tanjore. The entire credit of this marvellous transformation is not, however, due to Veranum. Owing to original defects of plan and construction, to subsequent neglect and to the operation of natural causes, his engineering had, in the course of centuries, lost much of its original efficacy, and for one of our own countrymen was reserved the honour of restoring, improving, and extending the work of the Hindoo rajah. Few Englishmen are better entitled to be regarded as benefactors of India than Sir Arthur Cotton, of the Madras Engineers. Of a daringly inventive genius, an ardent temperament, inexhaustible energy and unflinching self-reliance; fertile in expedients, prompt to devise, and eager to execute; sanguine in his anticipations of success, and a little too apt perhaps to exaggerate the success achieved—the very defects of his character only the better fitted him for the part to which from the commencement of his career he instinctively applied himself. He seems from the first to have considered it his special mission to aid in making known the hidden resources of India, and in promoting their development, and his success presents a very encouraging illustration of what may, in somewhat adverse circumstances, be accomplished by strong will coupled with strong convictions. Forty years ago, being appointed to the post of Civil Engineer in Tanjore, he found physical changes going on there which threatened speedily to neutralise the effects of Veranum's performance. Not long before entering Tanjore, the Cauvery is divided by the island of Seringham into two branches, of which the northern takes the name of the Coleroon, while the southern retains the designation of the parent stream. The former, having the more direct course and more rapid fall, received also from the outset a larger volume of water, and the inequality of partition became greater as in the course of ages the bed of one stream was gradually deepened and widened by the current, while the other was rendered continually shallower by the constant deposition of sand, until at the time we are speaking of, it seemed on the point of silting up completely. The consequence must have been the almost total ruin of the adjoining territory, which depends mainly for its irrigation on the Cauvery branch, the Coleroon serving chiefly as a drainage channel. Attempts had already been made to avert a consummation so greatly to be dreaded, and had not been without their use as palliatives, but it was left for Colonel Cotton and his coadjutors to apply an effectual remedy. This they did by damming up the Coleroon at the western end of Seringham, thereby diverting a considerable portion of its waters into the Cauvery, and by constructing in the latter a regulating dam which prevented the diversion from becoming excessive. The success of these and of some minor subsidiary operations was complete. The irrigation of Tanjore was re-established on a sound basis, and the prosperity of the province took at once a fresh start. During the next sixteen years the area of cultivation was largely extended, at least 50,000 acres of previous waste being brought under tillage, and the average produce per acre being increased by one-eighth; the land revenue of Government rose from 430,000*l.* to very nearly 500,000*l.*, showing a difference of 70,000*l.* a year, while the annual profits of the agricultural community were simultaneously increased by a sum one-third larger, and the selling value of their land was doubled. The cost of the works to which these improvements are mainly attributable cannot possibly be stated at much more than 80,000*l.*

A man of Colonel Cotton's restless activity could not of course sit down content with his achievements in Tanjore. Having 'scattered plenty o'er one smiling land,' he did not stay to 'read his history in *that* country's eyes,' but looked around for more space whereon to create fresh fields and pastures new, and he readily found what he sought in the Deltas of the Godavery and the Kistnah. The former of these rivers, rising in the Western Ghauts, within fifty miles of the Arabian Sea, flows in an eastern or south-easterly direction for seven hundred miles across the whole remaining breadth of the Deccan, and finally disembogues itself by several mouths into the Bay of Bengal, in the neighbourhood of Coringa and Cocanada, the only places on the Coromandel coast at all worthy to be called ports. We shall hereafter have occasion to speak of the capabilities of the Upper Godavery, but at present our business is only with the last hundred miles of the river, or with its course from the Eastern Ghauts to the sea. The territory there intersected by it is Rajahmundy, a province which thirty years ago, although possessing a rich alluvial soil, a fostering climate, and a convenient geographical position, presented for the most part an aspect of cheerless desolation. It was thinly inhabited, and cultivated only in patches; its population had been decimated by repeated famines, the results of alternating flood and drought, and the remnant of landholders, occupying fields which were now swept bare by devastating inundations, and anon baked hard by a relentless sun, had enough to do to keep themselves, and had little to spare for payment of rent or wages. The Government revenue, therefore, progressively and rapidly declined; and hired labourers, who were always paid in kind, thought themselves sufficiently paid with an occasional pittance of corn, together with an annual cloth to wrap round their loins.

The improvement which has since taken place is quite extraordinary. All evidence is concurrent on the subject. Rajahmundy is now 'a luxuriant garden:' 265,000 acres have been brought under wet cultivation, and the average produce per acre has nearly doubled. 'The crops are splendid:' nowhere else in India had Sir Charles Trevelyan 'seen such evident marks of advancing prosperity and personal comfort;' population has increased greatly, though it is still much below what is wanted; labourers are no longer at the beck and call of any employer, but have become somewhat fastidious in the choice of masters, insisting too upon money wages. The development of trade, both in imports and exports, has kept pace with the general progress, and fully a hundred per cent. has been added to the Government revenue. The *primum mobile* of a change so remarkable is undoubtedly Colonel Cotton. His ingenuity planned, and his diplomacy persuaded the local government to undertake works which, when once commenced, it has felt bound to continue at a cost far beyond what its over-cautious parsimony would at first have consented to. A brief description of those works may not perhaps be unacceptable.

It must be premised that the banks of the Lower Godavery have been a good deal raised above the level of the adjoining plains by silt deposited there during the annual overflow, insomuch that the river may be conceived as flowing along the top of a natural embankment, varying in height from 6 ft. to 24 ft. Across it, at Dowlaish-weram, between forty and fifty miles from the sea, is thrown an enormous annicut—a mass of stone and earth of dimensions suitable for bridling a river far broader than the Mississippi, and in the habit of rising every wet season 25 ft. or more above its usual level. The annicut is altogether two miles and a half long, 130 ft. broad at the base, and 12 ft. high, and the arrangement of its component parts is as follows. First, the descending current is arrested by a wall 4 ft. thick, on a level with the top of which is a horizontal platform, 4 ft. thick, and 19 ft. across, beyond which again is an inclined plane of 28 ft., slanting downwards. Wall, platform, and inclined plane are all of masonry 4 ft. thick, and constitute the external covering of the main weir, which is filled up internally with earth or sand. In advance of it, and extending 70 or 80 ft. down stream, is an apron of massy stones, on the stability of which the permanence of the whole fabric depends, for if the boulders composing it were displaced by the rush of water over the weir behind, the foundations of the latter also might be fatally undermined.

From behind the annicut the water, which by its means has been raised to a convenient level, is drawn off and distributed far and wide by canals adapted equally for irrigation and navigation. One runs to the established mart of Coringa; another to the neighbouring port of Cocanada; a third, after skirting and communicating with the Colair Lake, to Nursapoor, and others to other points of the coast. Altogether between 800 and 900 miles of artificial channel have been opened, from which water is first supplied to raise crops on ground that must otherwise have remained barren, and upon long stretches of which the crops so raised are afterwards carried to market, at less than one-third of the expense of any other mode of conveyance. Fifty thousand boats and rafts are employed in the traffic, lifting, according to a recent calculation, 870,000 tons annually over a length of 300 miles. Many additions must be made to the Godavery canals before the proposed system will be complete, but the area watered by them comprises already nearly 800,000 acres. When all are made, at least 200,000 acres more will be brought under their fertilising influence. Upon those at present existing, and on the annicut, about 620,000*l.* have been spent, a sum which has been repaid to Government more than twice over, and the present net annual returns from which cannot be reckoned at less than 25 per cent., to say nothing of the advantage accruing indirectly to the exchequer from the conversion of a herd of 'agrarian slaves' into a thriving peasantry whose well-being is attested not less by their independent bearing than by their abundance of food and clothing.

In the Kistnah Delta, the state of things, though sufficiently encouraging is not so unequivocally satisfactory. There too, at Bezoarah, an annicut has been raised, rivalling in Cyclopean proportions the one at Dowlaishweram; but though this, the most expensive item in an irrigational project, was finished many years ago, comparatively little progress has been made with the distributive channels without which the stream in rear of the annicut is arrested to little purpose. The soil, too, of Masulipatam and Guntoor, the Collectorates through which the Lower Kistnah flows, is of very inferior quality to that of Rajahmundry, and the quantity of water obtainable from the intersecting river is much less than can easily be supplied from the Godavery. Nevertheless, there can be little doubt that the Kistnah works have already fully repaid their cost, and some additional outlay is alone wanting to render the capital sunk in them a highly profitable investment.

While the Madras Engineers were signalising themselves by these splendid achievements, the Engineers of the rival Bengal school were not idle, but were engaged in operations equalling and even surpassing in scale those of their southern competitors. Between 1823 and 1843, Colonel Colvin and Captain, now Sir William, Baker, with the late Sir Henry Durand for lieutenant, re-opened the canals originally excavated by Firooz Toghlak and Alimurdan Khan,[1] which, after having been closed and almost hidden from sight by the accumulated drift of centuries, re-appeared under the name of the Western Jumna Canal, and now 'brood with watery wing,' and 'life and verdure fling' over an area of 350,000 acres. In 1848 was commenced, and in 1854 may, in a loose and provisional sense, be said to have been completed, the Ganges Canal, the value of which will be very inadequately appreciated if it fail to secure for the memory of Sir Proby Cautley, its principal designer and constructor, an Indian immortality. This, the most magnificent work of its class in the whole world, has a main channel 348 miles long, primary branches of 306 miles, and minor distributaries of more than 3,000 miles in aggregate length; in one place it is carried, by an aqueduct of fifteen arches, of 30 ft. span each, over a river 920 ft. broad, and thence for nearly three miles along the top of an embankment 30 ft. high. The area over which it diffuses irrigation is 320 miles long by about 50 broad.

In the Punjab, as previously mentioned, are many vast expanses of arid desert, which nevertheless possess

[1] *Ante*, p. 4.

within themselves or close at hand all the elements of natural fertility, and with a little aid from art might be made to blossom as a rose. In each of the Doabs or great tongues of land into which the province is divided by the five famous rivers from which it takes its name, strips of luxuriant cultivation skirt the limitary rivers, but all the intermediate space is an unbroken plain, producing little else than weeds and brushwood, and tenanted only by a few herdsmen with their sheep and cattle. Yet the soil is naturally rich, and if here and there a solitary hamlet can be found where a few wells have been dug, patches of tilled and garden ground are seen beside every hut, showing what, with proper treatment, might be made of the whole wilderness. Proofs are not wanting, either, that what might be has already been, for in many places numerous vestiges are met with of ruined towns, villages, and temples, and of dried up tanks, wells, and watercourses, which at once attest and explain the ancient populousness of the neighbourhood. Hints like these were not likely to be thrown away on local functionaries, among whom such men as Sir Henry and Sir John Lawrence successively occupied the chief places; and under the auspices of these energetic administrators, a work was undertaken, which, though not yet finished, is rapidly metamorphosing the aspect of the Baree Doab, the one enclosed between the rivers Beeas and Ravee. This is the canal which, leaving the Ravee just below the place where that river issues from the Lower Himalayas, and passing by the famous city of Umritsur, and thence through a desert of hard clay, overgrown with tamarisk bushes, will eventually rejoin the Ravee, after a course of 140 miles. On its way it throws off branches right and left to Kussoor, Sobraon, and Lahore, the length of which, added to that of the main line, will make the aggregate of the whole canal, exclusive of minor distributaries, 357 miles. The breadth and depth of the principal channel are as follows: at the head, 120 ft. and 4 ft. 9 in. respectively; after the divergence of the Kussoor branch, 92 ft. and 5½ ft. after that of the Lahore branch, 68 ft. and 4½ ft. Thenceforward, breadth and depth diminish, and at the place of rejunction with the Ravee they will be reduced by one-half, or thereabouts. The reason for such progressive contraction of dimensions is obvious. At Madheopore, where the canal issues from the Ravee, and where, to allow of its passage, a high stone bank had to be cut through for a distance of two miles, it draws off a quantity of water equal during the winter months to the whole volume of the river, whose bed at that season is consequently left dry for a certain distance, although a few miles lower down, as in the analogous cases of the Jumna and of the Italian Ticino, a stream, percolating the ground beneath, reappears above the surface, and with the aid of lateral affluents reconstitutes the river. Of the 3,000 cubic feet per second obtained partly at the canal head, and partly from auxiliary supply channels lower down, 500 will be required for each of the three branches to Kussoor, Sobraon, and Lahore, so that after the 55th mile, where the Lahore branch breaks off, considerably less than 1,500 cubic feet will be left within the shrunk sides of the main canal. The area expected to be irrigated is 650,000 acres.

As in the Punjab, so also in the adjoining Province of Sind, cultivation as yet is for the most part confined to the river banks, at a certain distance from which on either side commence what, though now a desert, was evidently once productive and well peopled, and might easily be restored to its ancient condition. In Sind, likewise, cultivation is dependent partly on the natural overflow of the Indus, and partly on artificial channels communicating with the river, and, when it is in flood, distributing its surplus waters over the adjacent plains. But though what are termed 'inundation' canals, are thus common to both provinces, those of Sind have some noteworthy peculiarities. Both eastward and westward of the Indus, but especially towards the east, some hundreds of them, large and small, are thrown off obliquely. Frequently they are well planned as to their general direction, but they are irregular in shape and irregular in slope or fall, and all possess one grand defect. Excepting at three isolated places, viz. Sukkur, where the river rushes through a narrow gorge in the limestone rock, Jerruck, where likewise there is rock on either side, and Kotree, where, though there is no rock, there is deep tenacious clay, the banks of the Lower Indus are composed of clay overlaying loose sand, which the current is continually undermining and transporting from one side to the other. The consequence is that the canals are continually becoming blocked up, either by masses of earth from the fallen banks which the set of the current throws into them, or by sandbanks, which the receding river leaves in front of their heads. Moreover, the periodical rise of the Indus is exceedingly variable, scarcely ever beginning or ending at the same time in two consecutive years, and exhibiting a difference in height of 2 ft., and sometimes even of 5 ft., in corresponding months. From these causes the quantity of water entering the canal differs by one-third in different years, while the quantity required for agriculture remains the same, and indeed ought to increase. The effect upon cultivation is that the farmer, who must always have his servants and cattle in readiness at the same period of the year, must often keep them in idleness until the inundation rises above the obstructions at the head of the canals, and must often sow too late or on insufficiently watered land, reaping subsequently only ten measures of rice or millet per acre, where, with a timely and adequate supply of water, he would have raised fourteen or fifteen. When the whole produce of the land is thus diminished, there is of course a corresponding diminution in the Government share, which is consequently exceedingly variable in amount. For instance, in 1853 the land revenue of Sind was only 284,000*l.*, whereas in 1854 it rose to 351,000*l.*, the explanation of the increase being simply that the greater rise of the river permitted more water to flow into the canals in the one year than in the other. The local government is not neglectful of a class of public works with the efficiency of which its own pecuniary interests are so intimately associated. Considerable sums are annually spent in giving an inward slope to the overhanging banks of the canals, in removing the rubbish where they have fallen in, and in clearing away the grass and jungle which, when left to themselves, soon grow thick enough in shallow places to choke up the passage. Every thousand pounds laid out in this way adds ten times as much to the Government revenue, and twenty times as much to the profits of the cultivators. Still operations of the kind can only be regarded as palliatives, and Colonel Fife, one of the most eminent irrigationists of Western India, in whose official reports the defects of the existing canals are very clearly explained, suggested many years ago what at first sight might seem to be a very effectual means of remedying them. He proposed that trunk canals should be cut, commencing at points where the banks of the Indus are composed of stationary materials, and running in a direction nearly parallel to the river, at a distance from it of about fifteen miles. Such canals would not be liable to have the shape of their openings changed by encroachments of the river, and would be less liable to be blocked up with silt or masked by sandbanks. Their supply of water would, therefore, be comparatively independent of changes in the river, and might be maintained when the latter was at its lowest level, and Colonel Fife considered that they might be kept always full and available for the supply of the existing canals, which they would cross at right angles, and which would serve them as distributing branches.

Colonel Fife subsequently matured the plans of which the above is an outline; embodying in them, together with his own ideas, those of some preceding labourers in the same field, and shaping them with a view not merely to the maintenance of the strips of cultivation (seldom more than from two to eight miles broad) between which the Lower Indus flows, but also to the possible extension of cultivation as far eastward eventually as the Runn of Cutch and the sandy borders of Jessulmeer. He projected four trunk canals: one from Roree, opposite Sukkur, which should run through Eastern Sind, crossing 150 inundation channels on its way to junction with a natural branch of the Indus, called Fullalee; one from Sukkur, which after running for about 100 miles in quasi-parallelism to the Indus, should rejoin the river at Sehwan; and two more, commencing, one at and the other immediately opposite Jerruck, and proceeding thence in south-easterly and south-westerly directions towards the sea. In apparent conformity with these proposals a canal from Sukkur was commenced in 1861, and the first 24 miles of it were opened in 1870; but according to the last advices it is 'silting up wholesale,' thus affording a confirmation, which I was very far indeed from desiring, of the doubts expressed on a previous page as to the wisdom of risking a large outlay on attempts to keep inundation canals, fed by the Indus, permanently supplied.

Here our descriptive catalogue must abruptly terminate. There are many other irrigational undertakings with interesting peculiarities well deserving to be treated of somewhat minutely, but space will not allow of more than cursory allusion even to operations of such magnitude as those which for several years have been carried on in Orissa for bridling the Mahanuddy and Brahminy, and compelling those turbulent rivers to fertilise the deltas which their inundations have for ages been in the habit of periodically devastating; or those which have quite recently been commenced for turning eastward a portion of the waters of the Sutlej, and thereby restoring to its ancient condition an immense area, once richly productive, but on which the desert has been fast encroaching since the streams which once enlivened it have either dried up or changed their course. Irrigation has now been authoritatively pronounced to be one of the prime wants of India; the Government has publicly announced the intention of devoting to its extension some twenty millions sterling during the next fifteen years; merely to enumerate the schemes in embryo, or in various stages of development, which have been devised in consequence, would be tedious, and would occupy time which may be better employed in a brief enumeration of certain questions affecting the general subject.

Of the great irrigation works constructed at the public expense, some few are abundantly remunerative, yielding to the exchequer, under the name of water rates, of increased rent of irrigated land, or of both, a very liberal percentage on the capital invested in them. Thus the Cauvery canals are reputed to pay $23\frac{1}{2}$ per cent. on their cost. The Godavery and Kistnah works are credited, somewhat extravagantly, perhaps, with 45 and 16 per cent. respectively; and the Western Jumna Canal probably pays quite 30 per cent. Of only a very few, however, can anything like this be said. In one single season, indeed, the rainless autumn of 1860, when other districts in the north-west were baked as if in an oven, the Ganges Canal saved grain crops enough to keep alive more than a million of people, who must otherwise, if left to themselves, have perished from hunger: saving the State too at the same time from the necessity of proportionate remissions of rent, and of a vast expenditure for the relief of insolvent tenants. But in ordinary years the direct net returns from the same canal average barely 3 per cent., while the Baree Doab has but just begun to pay 5 per cent. on a capital of 1,400,000*l*. and the Orissa works, on which nearly 1,200,000*l*. had been spent, earned, in 1872, no more than 700*l*. altogether, or not quite half of the same year's charges for maintenance and management. It may even be doubted whether, regarded in the aggregate, and from a purely fiscal point of view, all the irrigation works belonging to Government are not as yet a source rather of loss than gain; if those of the Madras Presidency be excluded, all the rest, taken together, certainly are. To prosecute its irrigational operations on the scale at present contemplated, and on the same principles as heretofore, may therefore seem to be a course that must inevitably involve the State in serious financial embarrassment; yet an opinion which has been for some time in vogue, and which, in the excited state of the public mind consequent on the horrors undergone by Orissa in 1866, and so narrowly escaped by Bengal last year, has obtained greatly increased acceptance, is that Government is in duty bound, at whatever financial risk, to extend irrigation to the utmost. The question thus presents itself how Government can best perform its supposed duty without danger of bankruptcy, and it has been suggested in reply that all the land capable of being directly benefited by any particular irrigation work should be held responsible for both interest and principal of that work's cost. Fairly enough, it is assumed that from all works of the kind, provided only they be judiciously planned and placed, and economically executed, an amount of good fully commensurate with the money laid out upon them may be immediately derived, and that the main cause why so many of them, nevertheless, appear to be financial failures, is the slowness of the people in the neighbourhood to appreciate the advantages offered. 'From time immemorial' the cultivators 'have used nothing but the water from heaven or from wells, and they are no more inclined to adopt a new system of irrigating their fields than they are inclined to send their children to school or to improve the sanitary condition of their villages and towns. In four out of five years the periodical rains are copious enough to give the people, if not all the crops that they desire, at any rate sufficient food, and the means of supporting themselves with some sort of comfort. During these four favourable years, when a canal has been newly opened, the people think very little about the canal water. Some of the more enterprising take it, and get rich upon it, but they are exceptions. In the fifth year there comes perhaps a failure of the rains, and the people suddenly find themselves on the brink of ruin and starvation. Then there is a rush for the water, and they find out its advantages. Some of them learn the lesson rightly, and take the water regularly in future. Others, when the pressure is over for the time, go back to their old habits until another failure of the rain occurs. Under our existing system, which leaves the cultivators absolutely free to take water or not, as they please, this is the sort of process by which canal irrigation gradually progresses.'[1] It has consequently been suggested that if, after a canal has been finished and placed in complete working order, the annual receipts from people voluntarily using the work be insufficient to pay interest on the money invested in the undertaking, and also to provide for the gradual repayment of the principal, the difference shall be made up by means of compulsory rates on all lands irrigable by the canal, whether actually irrigated or not.

That very cogent arguments may be adduced in favour of this high-handed policy may be seen at once on reference to the masterly State Paper by Sir John Strachey, from which the passage just quoted is extracted; still the objections to it seem to me greatly to preponderate. Undoubtedly if irrigation did really, as asserted, afford in the majority of cases 'perfect insurance against failure of rain,' and against the ruin thereupon consequent, it might justly be treated as a necessity which the Government would be at least equally warranted in forcing on an unwilling people as in requiring them to pay for the education of their children, for the drainage of their villages and towns, or the protection of their persons and property. Such, however, is the fact only very exceptionally—

[1] Observations on Some Questions of Indian Finance, by Sir John Strachey, K.S.I. Printed by order of the House of Commons in July 1874.

only in the north, where the Himalayan snows serve as inexhaustible fountain heads, and in the deltas of some three or four of the larger southern rivers. Everywhere else in India the rivers are themselves dependent on the precarious rainfall against the failure of which they are expected to provide. In few parts of the empire is irrigation more urgently needed than in Bundelcund, where the rainfall is peculiarly scanty, irregular, and uncertain, failing partially almost every other year, and once in every ten years or so failing almost completely, famine and pestilence thereupon taking its place. The local authorities are consequently loudly importunate in recommending that the Betwa and two or three other local streams should be irrigationally utilised so as to give, as they say, 'life in the midst of death;' but no statistics have been collected to show whether, when the tracts lying along the lower courses of these rivers are disappointed of their usual pluvial supply, the upper portions of their catchment basins do not remain similarly rainless, and whether, therefore, in the reservoirs proposed to be formed by damming up the rivers, water might not be most wanting when most wanted. If so, it would surely be monstrous that the cultivators to whom no vivifying water could be furnished in a year in which the question of their obtaining it might really be one of life or death, should yet have been paying for it, under compulsion, for years previously in which they would have preferred going without it.

Besides, even though nature were always propitious, the mistakes of art might counteract her favours. In

India, as in England, the most eminent engineers are now and then at fault. Six years after the Baree Doab Canal had been commenced, and after considerable progress had been made with the works, it was discovered that these had been designed for the carriage of a much larger quantity of water than could be supplied from the canal head. By the present Lord Napier of Magdala, when Chief Engineer in the Punjab, the *minimum* discharge from the Ravee at Madheopore had been reckoned at 2,753 cubic feet per second, whereas the *maximum* turned out to be no more than 2,529, and to obtain the full quantity required it was found necessary to make auxiliary cuts from both the Ravee and the Beeas, lower down. But, in the meantime, the upper sections of the canal had been excavated on too large a scale, and owing to this and other miscalculations, the estimate for the entire undertaking, which had originally been 530,000*l.* rose at once to 1,350,000*l.* In another instance, an expenditure of more than 40,000*l.* had been authorised by the local government for increasing the capacity of a tank near Madras from 55 to 196 millions of cubic yards, when it was discovered that the drainage basin which had been depended upon as the main source for the increased water supply, so far from being capable of filling the enlarged tank, had not, in more than one out of three consecutive years of actual observation, furnished more than one-fourth of the quantity needed to fill the old tank. Again, to combine navigation with irrigation has always been a favourite notion with Anglo-Indian irrigationists, but except on the comparatively short canals of the

Godavery, Kistnah, and one or two other deltas, the experiment has at best but very imperfectly succeeded. Scarcely indeed does it seem possible that an artificial channel, running for hundreds of miles in the interior, under a burning sun, should, in addition to what it is constantly losing by evaporation, be constantly giving out water for drenching the country on both sides, and yet retain enough to allow of the uninterrupted passage of cargo and passenger boats. It is probably in part at least for this reason that the number of merchant boats plying on the Ganges Canal in 1872-3 was only 239, having gradually fallen so low from a maximum in 1861 of 2,463. Yet in order to provide the imperfect facilities of which so little use is made, some hundreds of thousands of pounds must have been expended on locks, &c., proportionately increasing the cost of the canal and the amount of rates that must be levied to render it remunerative. Surely in cases like these it would be cruelly unjust for Government to compel the unlucky landholders of the district concerned to pay the penalty of blunders committed by its own officers.

It may indeed be argued that, however inadequate as a safeguard against famine, irrigation is at least a means, by availing themselves of which, the ryots could not fail, in ordinary years, immensely to increase the productiveness of their fields and their own consequent gains; that it is ignorance alone which prevents their availing themselves of this means; that if compelled to pay for water whether they used it or not, they would be sure to use it, and would thus at once learn a lesson of signal advantage both to themselves and the public at large, which otherwise the pressure of frightful calamities would be required to teach them. But want of water is not the only obstacle to the progress of Indian agriculture, which suffers almost equally from the deficiency and neglect of manure. Suppose, then, that the Government should at great expense place large heaps of manure within reach of every village—would it be warranted in compelling the villagers to buy the manure on the plea that it would be sure to be found on trial worth many times more than they had given for it? Would not such an interference with private judgment be as unwise as inequitable? Ignorance is always pig-headed; always bitterly resents being driven for its own good, and often stubbornly rejects the good towards which it is driven. That to attempt to force irrigation upon the people is about the surest way that could be devised of making it stink in their nostrils, has been proved by experience in Orissa. The authorities there began by dictating their own terms for irrigation. They are now doing their best to coax the ryots into accepting it by letting them have it temporarily almost for nothing, and promising that the present trifling charge of two shillings per acre shall on no pretence be raised for five years to come.

What now is the moral to be drawn from these premises? Even this, as it seems to me; that Government would act wisely in materially reducing its magnificent irrigational programme, or at all events in sensibly moderating its proposed rate of progress. Seeing that gigantic works, though they may pay well eventually, are almost always very slow in paying due interest on their cost, and that all that they meanwhile fail to pay is in effect so much added to their cost, the Government is in prudence bound to take in hand at one time only so many works of the kind as it can afford temporarily to lose upon. Not the less, meanwhile, may minor operations be vigorously prosecuted either by governmental agency or, preferably perhaps, by the village communities to be spoken of hereafter, or by any other associations of cultivators, that may be found or formed, with sufficient hold upon the land to encourage them to expend labour and money for its permanent improvement. For instance, mountain torrents and lowland rivulets may be utilised; both among the hills and in the plains reservoirs may be formed by throwing dams across ravines and narrow valleys. By such simple expedients, Colonels Hall and Dixon, forty years ago, brought the wilds of Mairwara under agricultural subjection, converting simultaneously their unruly inhabitants into an industrious, thrifty, and peaceful peasantry; and it is very satisfactory to note that the present Viceroy, Lord Northbrook, has lately advocated the adoption of similar measures in northern Behar, in preference to the too exclusive elaboration of grandiose schemes on the scale of those in Orissa, and that the Marquis of Salisbury has on more than one occasion, and particularly when recently addressing the Manchester Chamber of Commerce, delivered himself to much the same effect.

The only sufficient excuse for an opposite policy would be the fact of irrigation affording perfect insurance against famine; but not only, as we have seen, can it not do this, unless very exceptionally, it may, on the contrary, very probably aggravate exceedingly whatever famine it fails to prevent. For the larger the crops raised with the help of irrigation in ordinary seasons, the greater, probably, will be the population dependent on those crops, and the more numerous the sufferers in seasons of drought so excessive that irrigation itself is dried up at its source. In a country of such vast extent and such various climate as India, there is never likely to be a general failure. The whole country probably always contains food enough for the entire population, the surplus in certain parts being always such as would counterbalance the deficit in others, provided only there were adequate facilities for transporting it thither. A complete system of internal communications—of roads and railways, would therefore be India's best security against dearth. With it and irrigation combined, she might really be deemed fully insured against the direst irregularities of season. But irrigation by itself is liable to become a curse as well as a blessing, occasionally undoing in a single year all the good it had been doing in a previous decade.

Nor is this the sole drawback from the advantages of irrigation which, when unaccompanied by drainage, is apt to have disastrous effects, the exact converse of those which, here in England, our own effective system of drainage has once or twice inflicted upon us, and of which some tremendous visitation may not improbably ere long befall us, if we continue blind to the necessity of storing up water in winter and spring for the refreshment, in an exceptionally dry summer, of our burnt-up meads and gasping cattle.[1] In the neighbourhood of some of the canals of Upper India, and particularly of those led off, east and west, from the Jumna, have been formed vast pestilential swamps where, though rice thrives, men die off like rotten sheep; while other extensive waterlogged tracts have been rendered utterly barren by reh, a saline efflorescence, supposed to be caused by the rising to the surface, after dissolution by the canal water, of certain noxious alkalies contained in the sub-soil. The specific in both these cases is supposed to be thorough drainage, but irrigation thus supplemented might have its cost multiplied fourfold. After too much water has been brought upon the land, at an average cost of 12*s.* 6*d.* an acre, 2*l.* an acre more must, it is calculated, be spent in order to get it off again.

These evils, however, are preventible by suitable precautions, or remediable by subsequent appliances, and are trifles in comparison with others for which the ingenious author of a recently published treatise [2] is desirous of holding irrigation responsible. Actuated, perhaps, by some such feeling as that which led the Athenians to ostracise Aristides in disgust at hearing him perpetually styled 'The Just,' Colonel Corbett, of the Bengal Staff Corps, contends that the so-called blessings of irrigation are in reality

[1] 'Between 1868 and 1871 dry seasons prevailed, and the number of sheep in Great Britain fell off by 3,590,000, or nearly 12 per cent.'—*Board of Trade Agricultural Returns* for 1874.

[2] The Climate and Resources of Upper India, and Suggestions for their Improvement, by A. F. Corbett, Lieut.-Col. Bengal Staff Corps.

curses. 'What,' he asks, 'has irrigation done for the country?' 'Famines,' he replies, 'have been more frequent and more severe, since canals were made. Droughts are greater than they previously were; the air of the whole country is more arid and injurious to animal and vegetable life, than it formerly was . . . . Canals and irrigation are doing more than anything else to destroy the agricultural prosperity of the country and to reduce land formerly fruitful to a state of sterility.' In justification of these startling invectives, he explains that in Upper or North-Western India, to which his remarks more especially refer, the crops are divisible into the two classes of rain crops and cold weather crops, and that the former are reaped in October and November, after which time the ground commonly remains untouched until the rains set in about the middle of June, when it undergoes a shallow ploughing. During this process the constant treading of the wet ground by men and cattle consolidates the soil beneath the loosened surface, and forms a hard *pan*, which prevents the water from sinking lower. Repeated irrigation then turns the loose surface into mud, which plugs up the fissures formed below, and which, in drying, hardens into a crust of the consistence of sun-burnt brick, that reflects instead of absorbing heat. Off this firm surface the rain drains rapidly, while, through the cracks formed in it during the hot season, whatever moisture might otherwise have been retained is rapidly evaporated. Irrigation, he admits, in the first instance stimulates vegetation and increases the crops, but after a time, as the pan becomes consolidated, ploughing becomes shallower during the alternate soaking and drying of the land, and the earth's salts are raised from below by capillary attraction.

By way of remedy, Colonel Corbett suggests deep ploughing, liberal manuring, and the embankment of fields by ridges of earth. If the plough went deep enough to break up and pulverise the pan, the rain, when it fell, would sink into the ground, and moisture would not be raised again so fast by capillary attraction in order to be wastefully evaporated. If all vegetable refuse were buried in the soil, the retentiveness of the latter would be further assisted, and vegetation would not perish as it does when the evaporation of the leaves exceeds the amount of moisture taken up by the roots. If low ridges were placed along the sides of fields abutting on the roads, the outer ditches flanking them would have to carry off only the water actually falling on the road, and even this might be caught in shallow tanks here and there. If all this were done, Colonel Corbett believes that, even on unirrigated land, there would be nothing to apprehend from deficient rainfall, and no fear of famine. A scanty rainfall in any one year would not so injuriously affect the country, as the amount of moisture held in the soil by capillary attraction from the preceding year would be available for the support of crops, and, with it in reserve, a very small rainfall would suffice, insomuch that even sugar-cane, to which abundant moisture is indispensable, might be safely grown without artificial watering.

There is much of truth and appositeness in these remarks, and it is all the more to be regretted that Colonel

Corbett should have damaged a good case by exaggeration, and that he did not content himself with putting forward his proposals as supplementary to, instead of substitutes for, irrigation. No doubt, Indian husbandry is, as he has shown, woefully backward, and nothing that the Government can do for its advancement and for the diffusion of agricultural knowledge by means of direct teaching in national schools, and by the institution of model farms, ought perhaps to be neglected. But surely deep tillage, abundant manuring, and the ridging round of fields may be practised on irrigated as well as on unirrigated land, and would not lose their virtue by being combined with artificial watering. If improved husbandry and irrigation were really incompatible, and if it were necessary to choose between the two, the latter would, in spite of all Colonel Corbett's objections, greatly deserve the preference. No one who considers how often, even in our own humid and temperate climate, when there has been an extraordinary continuance of dry weather, green crops wither away completely on thoroughly ploughed and dunged land, can suppose that, under a tropical sun, the most skilful manipulation of the soil could of itself save them from a similar fate. In the controversy which Colonel Corbett has so needlessly challenged, the common sense of the ryots and of all others concerned will certainly side with Pindar and against him, gratefully acknowledging that there is nothing like water, and that even the water of canals is eagerly to be welcomed when that of the clouds is withheld.

Whether it is expedient in the construction of costly

irrigation works to permit the intervention of private enterprise in aid or substitution of State agency, is a question which at one time was warmly debated, but which has now been finally laid without much prospect of revival, and it shall here therefore be only very lightly touched upon. In the only instance in which the plan has been tried, that, viz. of the East Indian Irrigation Company—for, in the case of the Madras Irrigation Company, the element of enterprise was displaced by a governmental guarantee—it failed too completely to encourage the idea of repeating the experiment. The former company, after expending a million sterling on operations indispensable as preliminaries, but by themselves utterly unproductive, came to a dead-lock from inability to raise additional capital, so that the Government was fain to get rid of the obstruction presented by them, by buying up their property at a price far exceeding its market value. But even though the company's undertaking had proved a financial success, their interposition would still have been open to the decisive objection that all their private gain was just so much public loss. When a private landlord improves his estate at his own expense, all the benefits of the improvement are either appropriated by himself exclusively or are shared by him with his tenantry in whatever proportions his liberality may determine; but for any good done either to himself or them, he might as well leave the estate unimproved as suffer a third party to undertake the improvement as a speculation entitling the improver to the additional value thereby imparted to the land.

Now the Indian Government, although, in one sense, landlord-general of the whole country, is, in another, merely receiver-general of rents for the public for whom it is trustee, the whole of its income being presumably, and in the absence of malversation of every sort and kind, actually applied to public purposes. Of the profits arising from irrigation effected at the public expense, all that is not left in possession of the immediate tenants of the soil is thus virtually taken by the public at large; whereas, on the other hand, if the construction of irrigation works be committed to private enterprise, the latter's remuneration must consist of money which would otherwise have been appropriated either by the entire community, or by the agricultural section of it.

CHAPTER IV.

MISCELLANEOUS WORKS.

RAILWAYS and Irrigational Canals have detained us so long that we must run rather hurriedly over Miscellaneous Works.

Few countries, possessing so extended a seaboard as India, are so poor in good natural harbours. Some, and perhaps several of the estuaries by which the Sunderbunds are indented, deserve to be so styled, but south of Calcutta, along the whole of the Coromandel coast, there is not one, neither on the Malabar coast is there more than one, whose pretensions to be ranked in the first class have obtained practical recognition. Even Calcutta, though an excellent port when reached, is to be reached by ships, only after a hundred miles of intricate and often dangerous navigation, among shoals which continually threaten to increase, and which art has not discovered the means of diminishing. To bring a greater scour to bear upon the Moyapore shoal, spurs have been thrown out from the river banks, but these have lately been authoritatively pronounced to be a mistake, and, as a substitute for them, has been recommended a longitudinal training wall, nearly parallel to the left bank, 1,100 yards from it, and about 1,500 yards long. But to construct the wall would cost 150,000*l.*, and the Moyapore shoal, though the nearest to Calcutta, is neither the only one nor the worst to be dealt with. The Hooghly has so large a volume of water, its floods are so great, its bottom so soft, and the quantities of silt brought down by it so immense, as almost to defy attempts at improvement. 'The river,' says Mr. Robertson, 'is not one for experiments.' The menacing prospect held out by it for the future suggested some years ago the formation of a supplementary port on the river Mutlah, at a place about 24 miles south-east of the metropolis, where there is good anchorage for between 200 and 300 vessels of 20 ft. draught and upwards, and whencc a broad channel 55 miles in length, of a minimum depth of 24 ft. at low water, and navigable with ordinary care without a pilot, conducts to the sea. The idea was warmly taken up by the local Government of the day, under whose auspices a railway connecting the site selected with Calcutta was constructed at the public expense; but by the time the railway was finished, another Government, with other views, had succeeded, and declined to incur the further expense of embanking and draining on a large scale, and of the other preliminary works of reclamation, without which Calcutta merchants could not reasonably be expected to place on the edge of a jungly morass the buildings and miscellaneous accessories of various kinds indispensable for the establishment there of branch agencies, and for the removal thither of a portion of their business. The railway consequently has served for little else than to point a somewhat hackneyed moral. Where not only the entire *personnel* of the presiding Government is changed every five years, but where all the principal functionaries of all ministerial departments are changed still oftener, there can be no traditions of official policy strong enough to impart continuity of purpose to governmental action, and the abortive fate of the Mutlah Harbour scheme is but one among many instances of an undertaking commenced by one Anglo-Indian Administration, in order to be left half finished by the next.

Bombay, the one first-class harbour on the western side of India, ranks also among the very first of its class. Though almost land-locked, it is perfectly easy of ingress and egress: with 20 square miles of anchorage, it is capacious enough to contain many times as many vessels as are ever likely to seek its accommodation at once, and its bottom of tenacious mud is excellent holding ground. Moreover, the adjuncts which it requires from art are at length about to be supplied. Hitherto it has been utterly without wet docks, properly so called—of wet docks, that is, as distinguished from tidal receptacles; and all ships of any considerable size have to lie off at a distance of at least half a mile from the wharves, to and from which their cargoes are conveyed at great expense for lighterage, and still greater damage and loss from careless handling and wholesale pilfering. Now, however, a dock, after designs by Mr. Ormiston, sufficient for the reception of 26 large vessels, is on the point of being commenced on recently reclaimed land belonging to the local Port Trust; and this, which is expected to be completed in five years' time, may in case of need be connected with one or more additional docks, for which excellent sites, likewise belonging to the Port Trust, offer themselves lower down.

In respect of dry docks for building, cleaning, and repairing ships, Bombay, once upon a time, was rather celebrated. Some of the finest vessels of the old British Navy were constructed there, and it used to be one of her boasts that she could turn out two ships of the line, or one ship of the line and two frigates, every eighteen months. But in this age of progress the naval standard of magnitude has advanced like all else, and the Indian seas are now ploughed by iron Leviathans that can but just be squeezed into the largest masonry dock possessed by Government at Bombay. In the fine new dock, indeed, belonging to the Peninsular and Oriental Company, there is somewhat more than room enough for one of the huge transports that during part of the year arrive regularly from England with troops, but the vessel must unload before it can enter, and even then can enter only at spring tides, the foreshore of Bombay Island, where all the masonry docks are situated, being approachable by large vessels at no other period. The Government has wisely, therefore, set up at Hog Island, on the opposite side of the harbour, one of Mr. Edwin Clark's Hydraulic Lifts, which, though at first assailed by unaccountable local prejudice, is beginning to be better appreciated, and which, if properly utilised, will be found extremely useful at all times, and may render invaluable service in time of war or of other emergency.

India is not very much better off for secondary harbours than for those of the first rank. Foremost among the former is Kurrachee, two miles westward of the Ghisri mouth of the Indus, where very material improvements —for planning which almost the entire credit is due to Mr. William Parkes, C.E.—have been for some years going on. On Mr. Parkes' first visit to the place in 1856, he found the entrance obstructed by a bar, stretching across for nearly 6,000 yards, with a depth over it at low water spring tides of from 9 to 12 ft. By closing a passage through which part of the flood waters formerly escaped, constructing a groyne on one side of the entrance of the harbour, and a breakwater composed of enormous blocks of concrete on the other, he has produced an increased scour which, aided by systematic dredging, has cut through the bar an apparently permanent channel 500 ft. wide and 20 ft. deep at low water. Through this entrance, in 1871–2, passed 1,021 inward bound vessels of a total burden of 129,508 tons. Kurrachee is consequently opening, for the whole region to its north, a grand future in which it is itself destined to play an important part. Lord Lawrence, long ago, when Chief Commissioner of the Punjab, remarked that what that province required was not so much additional aids to production as a convenient outlet for its already superabundant produce, which in his day could scarcely be exported beyond sea without being sent to Calcutta. The Punjab and Sind may now thank Mr. Parkes for an excellent harbour, 500 miles from the nearest port of any sort on either side, and out of the track of the cyclones. To make it what it is has cost altogether about 450,000*l.*, and the money has certainly been well laid out.

In the Gulf of Cutch are two small havens, Poshetra and Seraya, and a third, Chuch Bunder, thirty miles east of Diu Head, all well sheltered, and with good depth of water. Little use, however, has hitherto been made of any of the three, and not much probably ever will be, now that the extension of railway communication promises to afford facilities for conveyance of the cotton and other produce of their respective neighbourhoods to so attractive an emporium as Bombay.

That Broach and Surat, at the mouths of the rivers Nerbudda and Taptee, should recently have been pronounced unimproveable is less surprising than that two such places, unapproachable as they are at most times by craft of more than 50 tons, should ever have been the seats of considerable maritime trade. Indifferent, however, as they are as ports, nothing better is to be met with between them and Bombay, nor below the latter until Jygurh and Viziadroog, both tolerable havens of refuge, are reached. Somewhat further south is Carwar, of which something has already been said in a previous chapter, and which, whenever it becomes the terminus of the projected railway there referred to, will doubtless become also the focus of a considerable trade. Behind the granitic headland, to which its existence as a port is mainly due, is a safe, though small cove, with a bottom of soft mud, where Indiamen used formerly to careen, and where and whereabout a moderate number of vessels may securely anchor during the south-west monsoon; and

Mr. Abernethy, by whom the capabilities of the locality have been carefully studied, considers that, by means of a breakwater thrown out from Carwar Head for a mile and a half, a perfectly quiet harbour might be formed, 4 square miles in area, with a depth varying from 14 to 32 ft.

Running along the Malabar coast from Buddagherry, in latitude 10° 35′, to Trivandrum, in latitude 8° 29′, at a distance of never more than a few miles, and sometimes of only a few hundred yards, from the sea, is a series of backwaters, which either already are, or easily might be connected, so as to form a continuous line of inland navigation 215 miles long, practicable by light steamers and other small craft. On the southern side of the entrance to one of these backwaters—a magnificent sheet of water, as large as Loch Lomond, in one part fully 10 miles wide, and generally from 10 to 20 ft. deep—lies Cochin, 'capable,' says Mr. Robertson, 'of being made the finest close harbour in India.' What he considers to be chiefly needed for this purpose is that, on the bar in front of the harbour mouth, with at present only 11 ft. of water over it, a powerful current from the 'splendid tidal reservoir' beyond, should be concentrated by means of two converging groynes carried seaward for distances, the one of 3,000, and the other of 2,300 ft. By this method he believes that a constant depth at low water springs, of 20 to 21 ft., may be obtained, and he is satisfied that '*every foot gained in depth over the bar will be retained permanently, and kept almost unvarying.*' Inside the harbour there is at present room for fifty ships of 700 tons each, if properly moored in tiers; but any amount of area can be got by dredging in the backwater, which, owing to the slightness of the rise and fall of tide, 'is practically a wet dock of greater extent than all the docks in Great Britain put together.'[1]

The English, having captured Cochin from the Dutch in 1796, thought fit ten years afterwards, in an inexplicable fit of blind fury, to destroy the fortifications and public edifices by blowing them up with gunpowder, at the same time so shattering the private houses by the explosion, that scarcely one of them of any size or value remained standing. An opportunity is now offered of making tardy reparation for this gross piece of Vandalism, by carrying into effect the measures which Mr. Robertson recommends, and the cost of which is estimated by him at no more than 75,000*l.* To this would, indeed, have to be added some three-quarters of a million sterling for a branch to Cochin from the Madras Railway, without which the suggested harbour improvements would be of comparatively little avail. The additional outlay, however, irrespectively of aiding to raise Cochin to the position, for which it is so admirably qualified, of commercial capital of Southern India, might not improbably, by providing the Madras line with a second terminus on the western coast, infinitely preferable to the wretched little port of Beypore, to which European vessels cannot get nearer than one mile and a half, occasion a fully proportionate increase of net railway earnings.

The principal drawback from the advantages of

[1] Reports on Indian Harbours. First Series, pp. 22–38.

Cochin is the difficulty of entering or quitting it during the monsoon, except on occasional days. In the worst weather, however, vessels cruising in the neighbourhood may rest in safety, if they can gain either of two remarkable refuges, the mud banks of Narrakal and Allippey, one five miles north, and the other forty miles south of Cochin, the account of which, given by competent eye-witnesses, reads like a passage in the adventures of 'Sindbad the Sailor.' Of the Allippey phenomenon, an old navigator of the seventeenth century says, 'It is a place that, I believe, few can parallel in the world. It lies on the shore of St. Andrea, about half a league out in the sea, and is open to the wide ocean, and has neither island nor bank to break off the force of the billows, which come rolling with great violence on all other parts of the coast in the south-west monsoon, but on the bank of mud lose themselves in a moment; and ships lie on it as secure as in the best harbour, without motion or disturbance.' Mr. Robertson, who visited the spot in 1871, says, 'We got into the boat with some difficulty at Allippey, on account of the surf; but, at the place where the bank now is, for several miles there was not only no surf, but not a ripple at the water's edge, and we stepped on to the shore from the boat with the greatest ease. Looking from shore towards the sea horizon, one saw a crest of surf, or, more properly speaking, swell, all round in a horse-shoe form, and reaching out to about three and a-half miles from land, enclosing this smooth pond—the swell being gradually deadened as it neared shore, till it died off into absolute quiescence.' Of Narrakal, the earliest account we have is that of a Dutch skipper, who saw it some time between 1774 and 1778, and describes it as 'a bay formed of mud banks, which extend to fully a league out to sea, and into which vessels may run with safety during the bad monsoon, and may lie in twenty or less feet of water, almost without anchors or cables.' 'A better description,' says Mr. Robertson, 'could not be given than this by a writer of a century ago, except that the action of the mud extends out to the six fathom line, and that the bank has shifted south to within five miles of Cochin.' 'There cannot,' he elsewhere observes, 'be the slightest doubt as to the tranquillising effects of the mud in stormy weather, nor as to the value of Narrakal (and Allippey) as natural harbours of refuge. No harbour in the world' (except Cochin) 'has such adjuncts. The existence and properties of the banks have been known for 200 years, and it is extraordinary that their advantages have not been more generally appreciated.'[1]

Along the whole western coast of India, from Cape Comorin to Calcutta, there is not a single spot where large vessels can be sheltered in all weathers. At one time, sanguine expectations were entertained with regard to Coringa and Cocanada, the latter of which, when visited by Sir Charles Trevelyan in 1859, promised, in his opinion, to become 'one of the most flourishing ports in Her

[1] Reports on Indian Harbours, pp. 39–44. Also a Paper by Mr. Robertson, extracted from the Proceedings of the Royal Society of Edinburgh, 'On the Mud Banks of Narrakal and Allippey, two Natural Harbours of Refuge on the Malabar Coast.'

Majesty's dominions.' But, whereas at Coringa there used, according to Horsburgh, to be 12 or 14 ft. of water over the bar at spring tides, there are now only about 9 ft. according to Mr. Robertson, who moreover found only 8 ft., 'diminishing rather rapidly to 5 ft.,' just outside the heads of the groynes that confine the channel leading up to Cocanada. The various mouths of the Godavery, in the immediate neighbourhood of which both towns are situated, bring down such immense quantities of silt into Cocanada Bay that 'in time the bay must become part of a delta.' Fortunately, to judge from what has taken place hitherto, in proportion as this transformation proceeds, a new and wider bay will be formed to the northward, affording anchorage 'preserved in its full depth, although pushed gradually further out.' It is to be feared, however, that, simultaneously with this process, the channel leading to Coringa will be gradually obliterated, and that access to Cocanada also may be eventually cut off.

While the Godavery is thus engaged in a work of destruction which threatens at some future time to deprive the fertile province of Rajahmundry of the only convenient maritime outlet for its abundant harvests, another river is performing a different office higher up. The copious silt discharged by the Mahanuddy at its embouchure a little below False Point, is fast extending northward a long narrow islet nearly parallel with the mainland, between which and itself a wider and deeper anchorage is consequently being gained. The harbour thus in course of formation is expected by Mr. Robertson to 'prove of incalculable value in the development of Orissa,' and is described as 'the most sheltered one on the east coast of India;' but the second half of this praise is not perhaps a very high compliment.

Along the whole extent of the eastern coast there is not, as has been said, a single spot where large vessels can be sheltered in all weathers; neither south of Coringa is there, with the exception of Blackwood Harbour, one where there is any shelter at all for them. Tuticorin, Negapatam, Nagore, Tranquebar, Cuddalore, Pondicherry, Sadras, Madras, Pulicat and Masulipatam are names which look well on the map, but the havens indicated by them can be entered only by coasters and other small craft. All other vessels must anchor in the open sea, where during the latter part of the year they would be exposed to the violence of the north-east monsoon, so that the few navigators who venture to lie off in that season must be prepared to weigh, to cut, or slip anchor, and work out to sea on the first setting in of a gale. At the best of times, too, a heavy sea rolls on shore from the Bay of Bengal, causing a tremendous surf which would infallibly dash ordinary boats to pieces, and which allows of communication between the shore and ships in the offing only by means of catamarans or of flat-bottomed and flexibly leather-like 'Massulah' boats, formed of planks, not nailed but sewn together with coir yarn.

The inconvenience resulting from these circumstances is especially intolerable at Madras, a city of 400,000 inhabitants, seat of the local government, and—although there is scarcely in the whole world a maritime town less fitted for it—seat likewise of an extensive and regular foreign trade. Naturally, therefore, the provision of better accommodation for the three or four hundred square-rigged vessels that, on an average, annually enter the roadstead and have to lie a mile or two from shore, has long been an object of local ambition. Ever and anon, wistful eyes are turned some 50 miles northward, to a fine sheet of water, 4 miles broad in the widest part, and from 5 to 7 fathoms deep, lying between the coast and the Armegan shoal, which latter protects it from the heavy ground swell from the east. By expenditure of a million sterling on a breakwater to protect it from the north also, this might be made really to deserve the name which it has long borne of Blackwood's 'Harbour,' but how much soever modern Madrassees may regret that the foreshore of this harbour was not originally selected as the head-quarters of their Presidency, they are not at all disposed to colonise it now. What they desire is to create at Madras some semblance of a Liverpool, not to create a Birkenhead that by its superior attractions may entice away the greater part of the trade of Madras; and with a view to the former object a closed harbour and a breakwater, projecting rectangularly from the beach, have been in turn projected. A serious objection to either is the danger of its being silted up by sand deposited by strong currents running along shore. The extent of this danger cannot be reasonably guessed, for scarcely as to either the littoral currents or as to the quantity of sand in motion, is there, says Mr. Robertson, 'a scrap of reliable evidence.' Be the danger what it may, however, it is at length about to be encountered. A close harbour, after designs by Mr. Parkes, whose well-earned reputation, based on his brilliant success at Kurrachee, justifies considerable confidence in any proposals of his of the kind, is about to be commenced, and will probably be completed in about four years hence. It is to be formed by two parallel piers 24 ft. thick, 3½ ft. above highwater level, and 1,000 yards apart, projecting 830 yards from the beach, and having arms at their extremities curving inwardly, and leaving between them an entrance 150 yards wide. An area of about 170 acres will be thus enclosed where it is expected that a number of ships, ranging from 16 to 48, according to the mode of mooring, may be adequately sheltered in the heaviest weather short of a decided hurricane. The harbour, however, is intended to serve less as one of refuge than as a gigantic dock where cargoes may be landed or shipped in smooth water instead of in the midst of surf, and by means of ordinary lighters instead of Massulah boats, an immense deal of damage being thus prevented, and much time and therefore money saved. It is calculated that altogether the expense of landing and shipping will be reduced by at least *2s.* per ton, at which rate the reduction on 275,000 tons, the assumed aggregate of imports and exports, will amount to 27,500*l.*; and it is further calculated that, in order to defray the annual expenses of the harbour when finished, inclusive of interest at 4 per cent. on its cost, a charge of very little more than half per cent. on 6,000,000*l.*, the supposed value of the aggregate imports and exports, will suffice. Not improbably it may be found impracticable to subject the entire trade to this tax, which could not reasonably be levied in respect of vessels that did not make use of the harbour, and, in that case, any deficiency in the expected receipts from port dues might have to be made good at imperial expense. But the Madras Harbour scheme does not depend for justification on the prospect it holds out of direct pecuniary remunerativeness. The risks which, in my humble judgment, may reasonably occasion some uneasiness are, first, that of the harbour (which, as seems to be admitted on all hands, must inevitably silt up sooner or later) becoming choked much sooner than its advocates expect; and, secondly, that through an opening of 150 yards, facing due east, dangerously heavy seas may gain admittance, in heavy weather, much farther within the harbour than is commonly anticipated. If, however, apprehensions on these scores should be proved by experience to be groundless, and if the harbour be really found to answer its purpose, its construction may then be entitled to be regarded as an enterprise in which, though it might have ruined private undertakers, public money has been profitably expended. For, irrespectively of their inestimable national value as guarantees against loss of life and property by shipwreck, the services rendered by good harbours are of the same nature, though different in degree, as those obtained from good roads or good railways. By facilitating access to market they increase the value of produce, raw as well as manufactured, and therefore that of land, and consequently, in a country like India, where the Government is landlord-general, increase too, indirectly, if not directly, the revenue of the State.

Serviceable in the same way are Ship Canals, which allow of long voyages being materially shortened. Of such canals, India possesses one, and projects have been mooted for providing her with a second and a better. The portion of mainland nearest to Ceylon is the promontory of Ramnad, separated by the Paumbum channel from the island of Ramisseram, whence a chain of rocks and shoals styled Adam's Bridge extends to the island of Manaar, which, again, is divided by only a narrow streak of water from Ceylon. For several years past, the Paumbum channel has been the subject of progressive improvements, and has been converted into a navigable passage from 80 ft. to 150 ft. wide, and from 11 ft. to 14 ft. deep, through which about 2,000 coasting vessels, of an aggregate burden of nearly 200,000 tons, annually make their way. To deepen it beyond 14 ft. throughout would be useless, as there is no greater depth in the approaches on either side, but either through Ramnad or Ramisseram a canal might be cut, practicable by the largest European vessels accustomed to ply in the Bay of Bengal. The cost of the operation is estimated at about half a million sterling, interest on which at 4 per cent. would amount to 20,000*l.*, but the resulting advantages might probably enough be worth the outlay. The canal would indeed be used almost exclusively by steamers, in whose case, however, the voyage from the Red Sea or Bombay to Madras or Calcutta would be shortened by its means by 350 or 370 miles, representing to a vessel of 1,000 tons, a saving of about 40 hours' steaming, and a total saving of about 85*l.* At this rate, to benefit to the extent of 20,000*l.* a year, would require less than 240 steamers, and the number of those that annually round Point de Galle on their way to Madras or Calcutta already exceeds 300, and is rapidly increasing.

Among Inland Canals several of those designed primarily with a view to irrigation, are, as already mentioned, intended to be used for navigation likewise, but cause has also been shown why, except in deltaic regions, the two objects are unlikely to be advantageously combined. Fresh water, too, is in most parts of the country too scarce and valuable to be spared in sufficient quantities for purely navigable canals, and such of these latter as exist are generally therefore replenished from the sea. One series, connecting the Pulicat, Ennore, and some other Lagoons, forms an almost continuous line of navigation for nearly 600 miles along the eastern coast from Sadras to Kistnapatam, and another gives similar continuity to the long succession of magnificent backwaters by which nearly the entire length of the Malabar coast is lined. Except on the sections nearest to Madras, by which considerable quantities of firewood and other necessaries are brought up to that city, there is very little traffic on the East Coast Canal, which, besides having to compete with the sea, traverses, during the greater part of its course, a poor and thinly-peopled territory. More use is made of the chain of navigable waters of the Malabar coast, at one point in which Mr. Robertson found 30 or 40 boats passing daily, and which may become of incalculable service during the south-west monsoon, in the event of effect being given to the measures recommended by him for raising Cochin to the rank of a great central emporium.

In one quarter of India, Natural Watercourses almost do away with the necessity for artificial canals. In the eastern districts of Bengal more particularly, the infinite ramifications of numerous rivers have immemorially served as a complete system of fluvial highways, which have prevented the want of ordinary roads from being severely felt. There is, however, no alternative but to accept them in the state in which nature provides them, for, in the vast alluvial plain through which they run, they defy all attempts to improve them or to forbid their continually deserting their accustomed channels and cutting for themselves fresh ones in new directions.

The Ganges and the Indus, likewise, serve as invaluable aids to commercial intercourse, but, among the rivers of central and southern India, the Godavery alone seems capable of being utilised for the same purpose. This is in many respects a noble stream, but its navigation is obstructed by three formidable barriers—at Sinteral, by two great masses of igneous rock, 4 miles in length, occupying the whole width of the river from bank to bank, and causing two falls, of 17 ft. and 13 ft. respectively, from the level of the water above to the level below; at Enchampilly, about 70 miles higher up, by a mass of solid rocks of slate extending for 10 miles, in which three falls of 13 ft., 15 ft., and 8 ft. occur; and at Dewalamurry, 75 miles higher still, by a multitude of rocks distributed over a length of 35 miles, which in many places is a perfect succession of cascades, and from top to bottom of which the total fall is 143 ft. A great deal of money has been spent upon these barriers, but with results very far short of what was expected. When operations commenced in 1861, confident hopes were entertained that an outlay of 300,000*l.* would suffice for the removal of all three barriers, and that continuous navigation for nearly 500 miles would be opened, during six months in the year for steamers drawing 6 ft. of water, and during two or three months more for boats of light draught. In 1871, however, after ten years had elapsed, and 700,000*l.*—considerably more than double the amount of the original estimate—had been spent, it was found that the first barrier alone had been overcome, that, for completion of the works at the second, 200,000*l.* more would be needed, and, after that, a yet further outlay of 440,000*l.* in order to dispose of the third, where as yet absolutely nothing had been done. It was felt, too, that even though, at the expense of not far from a million and a half, all desirable facilities for navigation should be obtained, the prospect of their being turned to profitable account would be very remote. The cotton and other exportable produce of the Central Provinces would probably take the shorter route by railway to Bombay, in preference to the longer one by river to Cocanada, where it would be much further from Europe than at first starting: coal from above the third barrier would scarcely be sent down the river in order to compete with the produce of the recently discovered coal fields in the immediate vicinity of the first barrier; and, although readier means of access might accelerate reclamation of the jungly solitudes intersected by the Godavery in its mid course, still India has just now many needs far more urgent than that of colonising an unpeopled wilderness. It was consequently resolved by Lord Mayo and the Duke of Argyll that, instead of despatching another 700,000*l.* in search of the 700,000*l.* that had already disappeared, the navigation works should be at once stopped, and suspended for an indefinite period; and there can be little doubt that the resolution was a wise one—the more so as the works can be easily maintained *in statu quo*, and readily resumed whenever altered circumstances may render their further prosecution advisable.

'The Lighting of the coasts of India,' says Mr. Markham, no mean authority on the point, 'is not perfect, is not even in so complete and satisfactory a state as that of Spain' (which, by the way, is exceptionally well lighted), 'or that of Greece; but a good deal has been done, and on the coast of British Burmah the system of lighting is admirable,' thanks mainly 'to the skill and energy of Colonel Alexander Fraser, C.B.' Mr. Markham proceeds to enumerate several places where additional Lighthouses are, in his opinion, requisite; in reference to which, and to the subject generally, I shall modestly confine myself to transcribing the following piece of judicious advice, tendered by the English Board of Trade:—'The Board desire to state, as a conclusion to which experience has led them, that in any body which is to exercise a general supervision over the selection and determination of the sites and characteristics of lighthouses, the nautical element should preponderate, for the sake of economy, no less than of efficiency. Engineering help may no doubt be needed (as in the cases of the Alguada or Great Basses), not only for the purpose of determining how to execute a given work, but whether it is possible or expedient to undertake it at all. But sailors best know what sailors want; and it may frequently happen that expensive works, which engineers and other landsmen think necessary, are repudiated by the practical experience of nautical men.'

India is intersected by nearly 16,000 miles of Electric Telegraph, whereof 5,285 miles are coincident with railway routes, and by nearly 32,000 miles of telegraph wire. The number of signalling offices is about 200. The tariff of rates for transmission has been the subject of repeated experiments. The present unit of charge is *2s.* for every six words, exclusive of five words of address accepted free, and this for any distance within Indian limits; and, as, of the whole traffic, about 40 per cent. passes between Calcutta, Madras, Bombay, Galle, Rangoon, and Kurrachee, places of which scarcely any two are telegraphically much less than 1,000 miles apart, such an uniform rate must be admitted to be moderate. It has, however, had less effect than might have been expected in stimulating traffic, the total number of messages in 1873 having been only 726,341, of which 100,612 were official, and 625,729 private. Of the latter, 66 per cent. were commercial, and 34 per cent. related to personal or social matters; 55 per cent. were sent by Europeans, and 45 per cent. by natives. The gross earnings in the same year were nearly 172,000*l.*, but the expenses of maintenance and working amounted to nearly 247,000*l.*, so that the debtor and creditor account showed a balance on the wrong side of 75,000*l.* The telegraph system of India must not, however, be judged by its pecuniary earnings. It is an indispensable administrative engine, which must be maintained at any price, and the Government must be content to accept, in diminution of that price, whatever commercial or social exigencies may constrain merchants and others to contribute.

The total expenditure of capital on telegraphs, from the commencement until the end of 1873, is reckoned at 2,730,000*l.*, or at the rate of 170*l.* a mile—a heavy rate, no doubt, in comparison with the corresponding average outlay in England, with which, however, it cannot fairly be compared. For, besides that some hundreds of miles of the Indian lines were, in the first instance, run up as temporary makeshifts, and had subsequently to be completely reconstructed—although not until after doing yeoman service during the Sepoy War—not only has almost all the material used in construction to be conveyed by a long and expensive sea-voyage from this country, but the material itself is of a much more substantial and costly description than that which is commonly employed here. In England, wooden poles suffice as supports for the wire, but in India white ants and atmospheric changes would make short work of these; and iron posts, therefore, are commonly used instead. The wire, too, is more than one-fifth of an inch in diameter, or nearly twice as thick and heavy as that which is found perfectly adequate here; and the cost of construction is further increased by the necessity of carrying the lines through numerous unbridged rivers, over mountains, and across wide stretches of desert or jungle.

As to the actual efficiency of the telegraphs, and the remarkable improvements wrought in them by the unremitting exertions of the present Director-General, Colonel D. Robinson, there are no two opinions. Colonel Robinson's management of his important department cannot easily be overpraised.

In addition to the telegraphs within its own territories, the Indian Government is owner of a submarine cable, laid down from Kurrachee to Fao, at the head of the Persian Gulf, and of a wire carried on iron standards along the Mekran coast from Kurrachee to Guadur, and thence to Jask; and it likewise holds, under a species of lease from the Persian Government, a line which, commencing at Jask, and proceeding through Bushire to Teheran, connects the Mekran Coast and Persian Gulf Lines with the Russo-Persian Line of the Indo-European Company. All these lines are admirably constructed and equipped, and are worked with an efficiency which leaves little to be desired in regard to either rapidity or accuracy of transmission; but, financially, they have all hitherto been anything but remunerative, owing to the competition of the Red Sea route, and the consequent division between two rival enterprises of a traffic that is not much more than sufficient for the pecuniary success of either. Now, however, a better era seems to be dawning. The Indo-European lines are capable of doing ten times the business they have hitherto obtained, and if, as is expected, one of the results of the approaching Telegraph Congress at St. Petersburg be a considerable reduction in the Indo-European tariff, a further result may not improbably be such an augmentation of Indo-European business, as will by future gains afford some compensation for past losses.

CHAPTER V.

PUBLIC WORKS' ESTABLISHMENTS.

By this term, in Indian official language, is signified the staff of functionaries of various degrees retained permanently in the service of Government for employment on public works. It consists of three divisions: the Engineer, and 'Upper,' and 'Lower Subordinate Establishments,' of which the two latter are composed of sub-engineers, supervisors, overseers, sub-overseers, sub-surveyors, and the like.

It is only within the last twenty years or so that the business devolving on these establishments has become largely developed. In the year 1849–50, the entire expenditure on public works of all kinds was no more than 600,000*l.*, of which 122,000*l.* was for roads, but the residue was devoted chiefly to the construction and repair of buildings, civil and military, and more especially of the latter, that is to say, of the forts, barracks, hospitals, and subsidiary edifices required for the European garrison of the country; for then, as now, the native troops were left to provide dwelling huts for themselves. The direction of public works thus came to be looked upon as mainly a military affair, and, as such, was entrusted to the Military Boards of the three Presidencies of Bengal, Madras, and Bombay, and their respective dependencies. With natural professional bias, the Boards, composed of the heads of the civil departments of the army, sought for executive instruments almost exclusively among their professional brethren, the favourite objects of their patronage being young Engineer and Artillery Officers, who had obtained their superior commissions by competition at the East India Company's Military College at Addiscombe.

Grand days were those for untutored genius, which however, as must in fairness be admitted, not seldom availed itself right worthily of its opportunities. At about the same age, and with about the same stock of the technical knowledge indispensable for the due conduct of public works, at and with which an Addiscombe cadet usually embarked for India, a young civilian, proposing to himself a civil engineering career at home, commonly enters the office of some eminent practitioner, under whose tutelage he continues for from three to five years. At first he is set to copy drawings and specifications, and to prepare estimates from working drawings, after calculating the amount of different kinds of labour and materials involved in the design. Next, he is directed to make finished working drawings from the sketches of his chief, and to apply formulæ to various constructions in masonry, brickwork, timber, or iron. When qualified to be of service in the field, he is employed in transferring ground plans of earthwork and masonry structures from the drawings to the ground; in boring to examine the nature of foundations or of materials to be excavated; in taking levels and running trial sections along a proposed line of road or railway. Thus he qualifies himself for employment as Assistant Engineer, in which capacity he superintends the execution of a work, seeing that it is prosecuted with proper materials, according to proper lines and levels, and otherwise in exact conformity with the contract drawings and specifications; and, even after completing his term of pupilage, he continues to be similarly engaged, being rarely entrusted with the planning and direction of any important work of his own, until he has acquired ten or a dozen years' practical experience by superintending the execution of the designs of other people. While, however, a young civilian of the last generation was thus slowly and painfully advancing, step by step, towards perfection in his art, his military compeer from Addiscombe, if ordinarily lucky, would have been running gaily along a royal high road to emolument and honour. Having completed the civil part of his technical training at the point at which the civilian was scarcely beginning his, he had gone to India and, being presently appointed Assistant Engineer, had been at once set to make roads and bridges, canals and annicuts. In Europe, a regularly trained Civil Engineer generally confines himself to one of these descriptions of work; but in India, a Military Engineer was presumed to combine in his single person the qualities of a Macadam, a Telford, a Rennie, and a Smeaton. At the end of a few years he would have become at least Executive Engineer, in charge of a district, and not impossibly Superintending Engineer in charge of a 'Circle,' with half a dozen Executive and Assistant Engineers under him and looking up to him, while by the local Government he would be quoted as a sort of oracle. Not that his reputation might not have been fairly earned and be fully deserved. The competitive examination he had gone through at College was a pledge for his possession of more than average ability, and this he had subsequently improved by scientific reading, and by a good deal of practice in making and correcting errors of his own, and in criticising those of his brethren. It was by men with no greater advantage of early instruction that the Grand Trunk Road from Calcutta to Lahore was formed, the Godavery and Kistna Annicuts raised, and the Ganges Canal carried through the air over one river 300 yards broad, through the volume of a second and under the bed of a third: it was from amongst such men that the Cautleys and Cottons and Baird Smiths emerged. These, however, were exceptions to the general rule, or, if they did constitute the rule, it was one attended by very many more exceptions than were at all necessary for its proof. Intermixed with the master-pieces of Anglo-Indian engineering there was, and still is, not a little of very indifferent workmanship. The traveller along the Great Trunk Road is still liable to be stopped by bridges that have either been broken through by floods not finding sufficient waterway, or that have sunk by reason of weakness of the foundation, or of some other constructive defect. On the Juggernaut Pilgrims' road, in Cuttack, 130 miles long, there are on an average more than two bridges to every mile, raised originally on arches so narrow that the floods, finding no sufficient passage, periodically overtopped the road, and damaged it to an extent which in a single year it cost 16,000*l.* to repair. Once upon a time, a navigation canal, from which great things were expected, was opened in the neighboorhood of Madras, but no sooner was it opened than it was reported to have been so ill-planned that to make it fit for its purpose would cost more than to cut another canal parallel to it, as was accordingly recommended. About the same time, in the Bombay Presidency, a newly-built bridge sank down through internal weakness, but not, as was naïvely remarked in the official report of the accident, through any fault of the officer who designed it and superintended its construction, and who, having had no previous experience in bridge-building, could not reasonably be expected to succeed the first time. To fall, as soon as built, indeed, used apparently to be almost a habit with some classes of Anglo-Indian structures. The Madras Government, commenting at no very distant date on the case of an arch of a bridge that had given way in consequence of having been raised on a foundation previously ascertained to be insecure, noted the 'remarkable frequency' of such declensions. 'Which fell down just as it was ready to be used' was an *obiter dictum* of Sir Frederick Halliday, when Lieutenant-Governor of Bengal, with reference to a fives' court erected for invalids at Darjeeling. Evidently, in Sir Frederick's opinion, the occurrence was too common to deserve more than parenthetical notice. 'I have known,' said a Bombay Executive Engineer, in a self-vindicatory letter, 'the works of many officers tumble down as fast as erected.'

Shortly before the virtual extinction of the East India Company by withdrawal from them of their governmental functions, the necessity of prosecuting public works on a much larger scale than previously forced itself or was forced on the Company's Court of Directors; and, in view of the contemplated extension of operations, regular Departments of Public Works were, in 1856, constituted in each of the Presidencies of Bengal, Madras, and Bombay, and in the Lieutenant-Governorship of the North-Western Provinces, displacing the old Military Boards, which were thereupon abolished. Some scores of Civil Engineers were also engaged in England and sent to India for service in the new departments. Of these recruits, who were somewhat hastily enlisted, and were selected mainly on the strength of testimonials, some turned out admirably—in proof of which it may suffice to mention that Mr. Leonard, now one of the Secretaries to the Lieutenant-Governor of Bengal, and Mr. Armstrong, holding a corresponding office in the Central Provinces, were among the number; but some, also, on reaching their destination, served chiefly to show how untrustworthy the most positive testimonials often are. One nominee was no sooner apprised of his appointment, by letter from the East India House, than he hastened to protest that the situation tendered to him was one which he had never sought and for which he felt himself to be utterly unqualified, having aspired to employment only in some inferior capacity. Another, having been described on high authority as combining 'the education of an engineer with the practical experience of an overseer,' and as calculated to 'prove a valuable acquisition to the staff of Civil Engineers,' was sent to Bombay on a salary of 400*l.* a year; but scarcely had he been tried upon actual work than his official superior was compelled to report that he could 'neither survey, design, nor estimate,' and that he was incompetent to do what even the lowest employee, on first entering the department, was expected to be able to execute. A third, in order to learn the rudiments of his profession, was placed for instruction under a native of the class of those whom he had come out to direct and superintend. Besides, even though there had been no danger of mistakes of selection, to send from England large batches of accomplished Engineers would, irrespectively of other objections, have been open to this, that it involved the continual supercession of men already in the Government service by others whom they would naturally look upon as interlopers. When, therefore, in 1858, the Company's administrative powers were transferred to the Crown, Lord Stanley, the first Secretary of State for India, resolved upon a new method of meeting the inability of the Indian military establishments to furnish a sufficient number of officers for the Public Works Department. It was arranged that a number of civilian cadets should be sent out annually, with not enough of professional pretension to warrant their objecting to enter the department at the bottom. These were to obtain their appointments by competition at yearly or half-yearly examinations. Lord Stanley's plan was acted upon for several years—from 1859 to 1868, both inclusive —throughout which period public notice was annually given that a certain number of appointments would be thrown open to competition. The invitation, however, was always very faintly responded to. In general the number of candidates barely exceeded the number of appointments offered, so that the competition was almost nominal, and the examination served merely as a test, and that of so exceedingly easy a character that more than average incapacity was requisite to avoid scraping through the ordeal. Yet the number of those who did manage to scrape through was, in only five out of twelve years, as large as the number advertised for, and in most of the other years was barely half as large, so that the Indian Government was compelled to make urgent requisition in 1867 for thirty, in 1868 for fifty, and again in 1869 for seventy more men from England, to be picked up as they best might be, in order to assist in designing, executing, and superintending the extensive undertakings in contemplation. Of course, of the men thereupon procured in more or less haphazard fashion, some were good, some bad, and many indifferent. Such was the state of the case when the Duke of Argyll, assuming the seals of office, became convinced, on looking into the matter, that the main cause of the failure of Lord Stanley's scheme was the want in this country of the educational facilities indispensable to allow of its succeeding—there not being at the time in the entire United Kingdom one single institution where the whole theory of civil engineering, or indeed where more than two or three of its branches were adequately taught.

Addressing himself at once to the supply of this want, and resolutely persisting in his purpose in spite of strenuous Parliamentary opposition, His Grace secured the establishment of the Indian Civil Engineering College at Coopers' Hill. The experiment was a doubtful one, but the felicitous selection of Colonel George Chesney as President of the College has caused it to be attended with much speedier success than its most sanguine advocates had ventured to anticipate. Not impossibly the brilliant example set at Coopers' Hill may stimulate the distinguished Civil Engineers deservedly looked up to as the heads of the profession in this country, to go and do likewise for the training of worthy successors to themselves. But be this as it may, there can be no reasonable doubt that Coopers' Hill, if protected against inconsiderate interference from without, will henceforth satisfactorily fulfil its present promise of annually providing as many thoroughly prepared civilian recruits as are ever likely to be annually required for employment on Indian public works, in addition to the young Royal Engineer subalterns annually sent out to help in maintaining the Indian military establishment at its prescribed complement. In common too with their military associates, the young civilians will possess much of the *esprit de corps*, the corporate sense of honour, and, what is part of the same thing, the dread of doing anything to disgrace their corps, sure to grow up amongst young men educated together with express view to their entering the public service. All the better spirits will certainly learn to take such pride in that service as will first ensure in themselves loyalty and probity, and will then, by the contagion of example, imbue their inferior companions with similar virtues. The gain which the Government will make by having its engineering operations carried on or superintended by men interested in their work for its own sake, and afraid of bringing shame on themselves or their companions by any unworthy conduct, is not to be calculated in money, though the mere money saving will be enormous. Nor will the public benefit arising from the existence of an exemplary body of Government Engineers in India be necessarily confined to that country. It is easily conceivable how the fame of their high character may extend to England, and contribute sensibly to the moral exaltation of the whole engineering profession.

Excellence in the separate components does not, however, necessarily imply corresponding excellence in the entire composition. A chain without a link that is not perfectly forged, may yet be too ponderous for ready use, and it cannot be denied that the Indian Public Works Staff has shown itself somewhat unwieldy. A great deal of first-rate work it has certainly done. There is no road in England or France to compare with the Grand Trunk, stretching from Calcutta to Lahore. There is nothing in Italy or Spain to match the annicuts and canals of Hindostan and the Madras Presidency, which as much outdo in scale and utility the dams and watercourses of Lombardy and Valencia, as the Ganges and Godavery surpass in volume the Po and Turia. Still, whatever praise on other accounts be due to the constructive faculty of the Indian Government's Engineers, it must be admitted to be singularly slow in bringing its products to maturity. Children who were looking on when the Grand Trunk Road was begun, had full time allowed them for growing up to manhood before it was finished. Though the Bezwarah and Dowlaisheweram annicuts were finished twenty years ago, not half of the distributing channels required for utilizing the waters periodically stored up behind them have yet been provided. For a similar reason, the Ganges Canal, though in one single extraordinary season it went far towards repaying its entire cost by the amount of good it did, does not as yet yield more than 3½ per cent. of net water revenue in ordinary years. This slow progress is commonly ascribed to want of funds and want of engineers, but it is in reality more largely owing to misapplication of the funds and engineers actually available.

The superior staff of the Indian Public Works Department consists at present of about 1,100 members, whose annual salaries and allowances, exclusive of those of their clerks, &c., amount to between 800,000*l.* and 900,000*l.* It is organized in this wise. The whole empire, from Peshawur to Rangoon and from Assam to Cape Comorin, is divided for official purposes into provinces, each presided over by a Chief Engineer, and subdivided into between 30 and 40 circles, over which Superintending Engineers preside, each with a dozen or so of Executive and Assistant Engineers under him. The specific duty of these officers is to keep in repair the roads, canals, bridges, barracks, jails, &c., with which their province, circle, or district is already provided; to ascertain what additional ones are required; to make designs and estimates for these latter, and to carry into execution such plans as they can obtain sanction for. Not perhaps an ill-devised organization this, with reference to its purpose, provided there were adequate motive power to keep it going. Such immense machinery, however, evidently requires immense pecuniary steam, and though the Indian Government has for years past been spending at the rate of five, six, or seven millions a year on public works, still even that expenditure is insufficient to allow of public works proceeding at the rate of speed desirable over the whole of India simultaneously. Since, however, there the machinery is, it cannot be suffered to stand idle and grow rusty from disuse. Since there the several provincial establishments are, threatening to eat their heads off if left without something to do, some employment must be given to every one of them, sufficient to produce at least some show of activity. So funds, which if devoted exclusively to the prosecution of one or two important works, would have caused them to be finished off-hand, are frittered away by being distributed amongst a dozen or more; and the consequence is that, at the close of every working season, instead of 100 miles of new road or new canal straight on end in any one direction, there are a dozen or more of disjointed portions connected with nothing and leading nowhere. Rather than allow the inhabitants of one district to have improved means of locomotion or of irrigation earlier than those of another, half a dozen districts are all kept waiting to have their wants in those respects supplied, as long as the latest served would have had to wait if they had been attended to one after the other instead of all at once. On the other hand, if in aid of any work of extraordinary urgency an extraordinary grant be made, then it not unfrequently happens that the whole of the grant cannot be utilized within the year, owing to the want of engineers. There is always a lack of these where there is much for them to do, because so many of them are scattered about in places where there is little to be done. Where money is plentiful, work is delayed for want of engineers; where engineers are present in sufficient number, work languishes for want of money. A partial remedy for this double evil would obviously be greater concentration of resources of both kinds. However proper it may be to station permanently two or three engineers in each province, it is obvious that if all the rest were held *en disponibilité*, constantly ready for immediate despatch whithersoever full employment could be afforded them, not only might all work undertaken be prosecuted with much greater vigour and brought much earlier to conclusion, but a much smaller number of persons would suffice for its superintendence. Most assuredly, if a great private firm, like that of the late Mr. Brassey, were to take a contract for six or seven millions' worth of work, it would not devote anything like 800,000*l.* to salaries of superintendents, over and above the amount required for wages of labour, skilled and unskilled.

That the constitution of the Indian Public Works Department is very far from perfect is tacitly admitted by the partial remodelling and reform which it is continually undergoing at the hands of the local Government;

but hitherto reform has signified, not simplification, but complication; not concentration, but multiplication of offices. A wise private employer understands that he cannot get the best service out of the best servants without trusting them sufficiently to allow of their exercising considerable latitude of discretion. He may summarily discharge his gardener or his coachman if he suspects him of extravagance or dishonesty; but as long as he retains either, he leaves the one to judge when, and what fires are needed in the hot-houses without standing over him to see how much fuel is used; neither does he go into the stables whenever the horses are fed, in order to prevent the other from stealing the corn. But Governments in general, and the Indian Government in particular, behave as if they believed all their servants to be knaves, only to be kept from picking and stealing by being sharply and suspiciously watched. In constituting the Indian Public Works Department, the aim seems to have been less to stimulate than to control activity, for which latter purpose a regular gradation of checks has been created; and it seems also to have been imagined that the force of control would be augmented by being arrested at a series of barriers, and filtered through a series of sieves. The supreme controlling authority being lodged with the Governor-General and his Council, next in order comes, as administrative head, a Secretary to Government, having under his immediate control the Chief Engineers of provinces, below and controlled by whom are the Superintending Engineers of circles, who in turn control Executive Engineers of districts, to whose control finally the Assistant Engineers are immediately subject. All this may be proper, and indeed almost indispensable, as long as the present provincial distribution of establishments subsists, but close beside and of co-ordinate authority with the provincial Chief Engineers, stand Inspectors-General of Military, of Civil, and of Irrigation Works, each controlling a separate staff of Superintending, Executive, and Assistant engineers. There is also a distinct staff for State Railways, for though it was for a while deemed sufficient that the Engineer in principal charge of each of these should, without prejudice of course to his ulterior controlability by the Government, be placed under the immediate control of the Secretary to Government—a Deputy Secretary, an Under Secretary, and an Assistant Secretary, all specially for railway business, being thereupon created—it has latterly been deemed expedient to interpose between the Government Secretariat and the Chief Engineers of State Railways, a new controlling authority, composed of a Director and Assistant Director. These functionaries, be it observed, have nothing to do with the preliminary investigation of projects; they are not to be called upon to give opinions on engineering questions, nor yet, after a line has been completed, are they to ascertain by personal examination whether it has been properly constructed—those duties being expressly reserved for a separate officer, the Consulting Engineer for State Railways. Their business consists chiefly of supervision of constructive operations while the railway is being made, and of that of repair, maintenance, and traffic operations after it is opened.

Now, in India, the Governor-General and his Council stand in precisely the same relation to a State railway as a Board of Directors does in England to the line of a railway company. In both countries, before constructive operations are commenced, plans and estimates, framed with whatever minuteness of detail is deemed desirable, must receive the sanction of the supreme authority, but that sanction having been accorded, and limits thereby set which the Chief Engineer is bound at his peril not to transgress, he is in England left to move freely within those limits with the least possible let or hindrance. Presumably, he has been selected for his post as being the fittest person available for it, the one best qualified by professional knowledge and skill, integrity and administrative ability. Having then been fully instructed as to what is required of him, he is suffered to judge for himself how best to carry out his instructions, with a tacit understanding between himself and his employers that his conduct of affairs shall be judged by the result. Within the scope of a defined project, he is allowed free play for his talents; it is chiefly when he has some alterations of plan to propose that he need refer to his directors for further guidance or additional powers. But in India, not only has the Engineer in charge of a State railway no communication with the Government, not only must all his representations and suggestions be addressed to an intermediate Director or Deputy Director, with whom it rests to determine whether or not to pass them on, and to modify them as he pleases on their passage, he must also, even in the performance of his prescribed duties, pause at every stage to report progress to the same intermediaries, in order that these may decide whether he is proceeding aright, and shall be allowed to proceed further. Without their permission no separate item of an aggregate estimate which the presiding Government has already passed, can be acted upon; every separate design and specification must have their approval, every draft upon the Government treasury must have their endorsement. Swathed round so tightly with coils of red tape, the veriest engineering Samson would become helpless. To what end have his services been engaged, if he is to be denied the free use of his faculties?—denied the confidence which, when worthily bestowed, tends above all things to elicit zeal and public spirit, and treated instead with a show of jealousy and suspicion than which nothing is so apt to engender precisely those frailties against which it is designed to guard? And what is the supposed efficacy of all this extra vigilance? Even though the Railway Engineer requires to be so closely watched, who is to watch the watchers? After all, the ultimate supervision remains with the Government, but is the Government likely to see more clearly for looking through the Director's spectacles instead of through its own eyes? The Director may possibly be superior to the Engineer in capacity and integrity, but possibly too he may be only equal, or even inferior. If superior, his appropriate place is that of the Engineer; it is he who ought to have been placed in charge of a business which he best understands. But if only equal, he is at best but an useless encumbrance, while, if inferior, the better judgment is compelled to defer to the worse.

Interwoven with the general network of official forms by which the operations of the Public Works Department are hampered, is a sub-reticulation, entitled to a few words of separate notice. For many years to come the expenditure of the department will probably continue to be as at present, about eight or nine millions sterling annually, of which amount rather more than a million is at present absorbed by the salaries and wages of the superintending staff, viz., 810,000*l.* by Engineers of various grades, and 216,000*l.* by 'Upper Subordinates.' If 'Lower Subordinates,' clerks, travelling expenses, and contingencies be added, the total charge for superintendence will rise to a million and a half. But over and above all this, nearly 150,000*l.* a year is spent upon mere book-keeping. There are first 311 Accountants with salaries ranging from 96*l.* to 540*l.* a year, by whom the accounts are kept; and then, presiding over these, a hierarchy to whom the accounts when compiled are submitted for audit, consisting of one Accountant-General at 3,000*l.* a year, one Deputy Accountant-General at 1,320*l.*, one Assistant Accountant-General at 1,140*l.*, nineteen Controllers of Accounts, with salaries ranging from 720*l.* to 1,920*l.* a year, thirteen Deputy Controllers at 660*l.* each, and ten Assistant Controllers at from 300*l.* to 540*l.* per annum. Of these superior functionaries, nine are Royal Engineer Officers, to wit, two lieutenant-colonels, five captains, and two lieutenants, besides one major, one captain, and two lieutenants of the Staff Corps, whose scientific attainments have been tested and certified at the Engineering College at Roorkee. Now, not to speak of the waste of power[1] implied by such employment of such accomplished instruments, the question naturally arises whether the numerical strength so applied is not far greater than necessary. Can it be doubted that many trained accountants in the City of London would be able, if called upon, to devise a system of account and audit equally efficient, and much simpler and more economical? The entire expense of the Audit Office at Somerset House, by which are supervised the accounts, not of Public Works only, but of the whole public expenditure of every sort of the United Kingdom, amounts to less than 44,000*l.* a year.

The many-storeyed fabric of control referred to above has quite recently received its crown by the appointment of a new member to the Governor-General's Council, whose especial charge is to be the affairs of the Public Works Department. This is a measure which it may perhaps seem unbecoming in me to criticize, but its chief author and originator belongs to that higher order of minds which court rather than discourage the undisguised expression of opinions opposed to their own; and I have therefore no fear that Lord Salisbury will resent the respectful freedom of the few following observations.

[1] The versatile talents of Colonel George Chesney, the accomplished author of that excellent manual for Indian statesmen, his Treatise on 'Indian Polity,' were for some years confined within the narrow official sphere of Accountant-General for Public Works.

The body most nearly analogous to the Indian Vice-regal Council is perhaps the English Ministerial Cabinet, but, together with considerable likeness, there are also some essential differences between the two. Most of the members of the Cabinet are also heads of great Departments of State, in conducting the business of which each is left pretty much to his own discretion, his colleagues never thinking of interfering with details which he is reasonably assumed to understand better than they, and he seldom or never referring to his colleagues except when some large question of State policy is concerned. Thus the collective deliberations of the Cabinet are presumably restricted to the main stream and wider currents of governmental action. Attention to these is likewise the chief duty of the Indian Council, the more especially as only two of its members, the Commander-in-Chief and the Financc Minister, are in any sense heads of departments—all the others, even the Legislative member, being what in Continental phrase are termed ministers without portfolios, whose principal vocation is to join in the Viceroy's deliberations, and to advise him upon topics of Imperial moment. As, however, the majority of departmental chiefs are without seats in the Council, it is unfortunately indispensable that these, unless they are to be virtually independent of the central Government, should submit their proceedings to it for confirmation, and accordingly great part of the business of the Council consists in passing orders on the proceedings so submitted. In determining, however, what those orders should be, the Council clearly ought to act collectively. Division of labour is here altogether out of place— not unnecessary merely, but, in so far as it exists, decidedly prejudicial. For in the first place, the labour to be performed is not very great, since, unless the executive heads of departments are very unfit for their posts, confirmation of their proceedings must be to a great extent a mere matter of form; and in the second, when approval of their proceedings is open to question, if examination of the question be primarily delegated to a particular Councillor, the final decision upon it will, in nine times out of ten, be that same Councillor's. Already, in regard to military and financial affairs, the Governor-General, consciously or unconsciously, no doubt defers greatly to the Commander-in-Chief and to the Financial Councillor, in consideration of the special attention which these are assumed to have given to those affairs; and if all other governmental business, diplomatic and domestic, legislative and administrative, were divided amongst the other councillors, the Governor-General would presumably, for the same reason defer similarly to them, so that, unless he had reserved some particular branch of business to himself, he would be reduced to a comparative cipher. It would seem then that to the councillor who will henceforward be required to attend particularly to Public Works, will belong the chief direction and control of those works. It will therefore be his duty to review regularly and minutely all the proceedings of the Public Works Secretary to Government, who has hitherto been the executive chief of the Public Works Department; it will be his duty, in fact, to do over again all that the Secretary has already done. Now he may be either equally or better qualified than the Secretary to do the Secretary's work, or he may be less qualified ; he may be able to do it as well, or better, or he may be unable to do it as well. If equally or more able, there will be no use in maintaining the Secretary as well as the Councillor: the former functionary's services may be dispensed with and his salary saved, while, on the other hand, if the Secretary's be the superior capacity, the better judgment will be liable to be overruled by the worse. It may be said that the Secretary has at present not sufficient authority over his department, but if so the appropriate remedy would seem to be to increase his authority. If it be deemed essential that the Public Works Department should be represented in the council, either the Secretary might have a seat there, becoming in that case the counterpart of an English Secretary of State, or the Councillor, when not engaged in council, might take the Secretary's place at office. Both, however, can scarcely be needed, and there seems reason to apprehend that to have retained the Secretary and to have superadded a Councillor may be found to have encumbered a machine, already sufficiently complex and expensive, with a superfluous and costly additional cog-wheel.

This chapter must not conclude without some notice of the 'Upper and Lower Subordinate Establishments,' in speaking of which, however, I shall, for reasons, confine myself to some observations for the substance of which I am indebted to my friend Mr. Leonard, C.E., one of the Secretaries to the Government of Bengal.

Both establishments are composed mainly of passed pupils from the indigenous Engineering Colleges, where a number of aspirants to the inferior class of supervising appointments are always in training; some of them being British non-commissioned officers or privates, and the remainder young civilians—for the most part native lads. 'But,' says Mr. Leonard, 'I know of no country beside India, where the only qualification required from an overseer—that is, from the man who has practically to get the work done—is purely theoretical knowledge. In most countries, a man is made an overseer because he is a thoroughly good workman, or because, being a fair workman, he is unusually smart as a manager, quick in contriving, neat in arranging, or has some such special qualification; but here the only qualification required is such as a man can attain, and does attain, without ever having seen a rupee's worth of work done, or ever having shown the slightest aptitude for contrivance or management, or even any bent for the particular line which he has chosen beyond the bent to earn a living as easily as he can. A lad of this sort passes his examination in college, is posted to a division, and straightway is sent to an out-station to build a set of sub-divisional buildings, to make a road, or to build a bridge, perhaps. No wonder then if we have to complain of bad work, if we are cheated, and if progress is often slow.'

On Bengalee lads more particularly, who are always fond of showing off their acquirements, even in the most inappropriate circumstances, the theoretical smattering picked up at college is apt to have an injurious effect—

puffing up instead of edifying. A clever young overseer, who was putting up a spur at Bamunghatta to save the toll-house from being cut away by the action of the river, on being shown by Mr. Leonard that he had not done it as he had been told, and that it would not protect the bank, produced, by way of reply, a paper covered with algebraic signs to demonstrate that it was in the proper position for resisting the current, although, as he admitted, it would be of no use to the bank.

If some practical training is to be required as an additional qualification from these 'very theoretical young Bengalees,' changes in the present preliminary education must, in Mr. Leonard's opinion, be made, and the standard for admission into the department lowered, since 'it would be too much to expect the same theoretical knowledge as is now exacted, and a good practical training as well.' His idea is that a 'Public Works Subordinate School' should be established, into which entrance should be obtained by the passing of certain easy tests, limited to a tolerable knowledge of English, and a fair acquaintance with arithmetic and mathematics, and where the pupils should be taught simple surveying, plan drawing and estimating, and easy practical mechanics, being then sent out as apprentices to learn practical work. With a view to instruction in this latter, he proposes that divisions, in which useful work was going on, should be selected and changed from time to time, and that to each division should be attached a thoroughly good subordinate, with nothing to do but to take charge of the pupils and teach them to work. To assist him in doing this, certain projects might be made over to him by the Executive Engineer, to be carried out exactly as if they were being done by contract, and on these the pupils should be made to labour with their own hands so far as might be necessary for rendering them thoroughly acquainted with the nature of good work, and of the art of doing it.

These suggestions seem to speak sufficiently for themselves. The only amendment which I shall presume to move upon them is that the proposed new school be dispensed with, and that the instruction proposed to be given there be given instead in special classes organized for the purpose in the Engineering Colleges at Roorkee and elsewhere.

CHAPTER VI.

LAND TENURE.

'I HAVE mentioned,' says Lieutenant-Colonel Haig, in a recent report on the irrigation of Orissa drawn up by him in the capacity of Chief Engineer in Bengal, 'I have mentioned that the zemindars are raising the rents of irrigated lands. There is no doubt that this is extensively the case; probably universally so wherever irrigation has become at all established. The rents have risen generally only from *6d.* to 1*s.* per acre,[1] but in some places much more. I was shown a large tract of sandy land, for which the rent per acre used to be 3*s.* 1½*d.*, and is now, since irrigation has been brought in, 8*s.* Some ryots of another township complained of the zemindar having raised the rents from 2*s.* to 8*s.* In some places the high and light soils have been so enriched by the silty canal water that the ryots themselves have raised the rents by competition from 3*s.* 1½*d.* to 7*s.*; and I passed through a considerable extent of newly cleared and irrigated land for which the zemindars now charge

[1] Here, as elsewhere, I have turned Indian into English money, and Anglicised some Indian words.

6*s*. or 8*s*. an acre, though it was covered with jungle before the distributary was made through it. The waste lands, which are only to be found on the tops of the ridges on which the distributaries run, are everywhere being taken up for cultivation, and the zemindars get for them, almost immediately, the same rents as they charge for the low lands and the hollows. It seemed to me to be almost a question whether it might not be better to refuse water for the cultivation of waste lands, than, by giving it at only 2*s*., to sacrifice almost the whole of the profit to the zemindars. It is quite evident that at least 4*s*., if not 6*s*., would be readily paid for water for such lands. The process of conversion is so rapid, and the competition so keen that, four years hence, I fear the greater part of the waste will have been reclaimed, and the rents raised to such a degree as to leave but a small margin for water rate.

'The same result, though in a less degree, will certainly follow the irrigation of all other lands not held under fixed rents. Judging by present appearances, it seems certain that, when the time comes to revise the present scale of water rates, the ryots will be found to be paying generally from one to two shillings more rent for their land than now, and that by so much must the increased water rates which might otherwise have been charged be reduced. A large share of the profits from irrigation will go into the pockets of the zemindars, who will not return a single rupee of them to the State, to the ryots, or to the land in any shape whatever. There are soils which, though of little value without water, become so enriched by it as to bear several times their former rent. This is true of all the light and sandy soils, the rents of which without water are usually from 2*s.* to 2*s.* 6*d.*, and with it become 8*s.* and more. It must surely be a mistake to make the same charge for water for such lands as for others lower down which pay 8*s.* already. Water may be not worth more than 2*s.* or 2*s.* 6*d.* to the latter, while to the former it is worth 6*s.* or 8*s.* If the State does not make a corresponding charge for the canal water, the only result will be that the zemindars will take the difference in the shape of rent. The ryots will pay the same in either case, but, with an uniform rate, three-fourths of the profits will fall to the zemindars.'

I have extracted these passages, well meriting quotation on other accounts, because they may serve to show how intimate in India is the connection between public works and the tenure of land, and how incomplete would be any treatise on the former subject which did not include a section devoted to the latter. Public works profess to have in view the good of the public at large, but in India the bulk of the population is agricultural, and the extent to which agriculturists can share in the advantages of public works depends mainly on the conditions on which they are permitted to hold the land they cultivate. Railways, by opening access to new markets and by rendering old markets more readily and cheaply accessible, may cause land to be more extensively and more skilfully cultivated, and irrigation may double or quadruple the fertility of the soil, but mere increase of produce will avail little to the peasantry, except in so far as the rules of distribution in force permit part of the increment to remain in their possession; and the rules of distribution bearing on that particular point are identical with the obligations imposed by the owners of the soil on its occupiers and tillers. Now in India, these obligations vary exceedingly, but it is scarcely too much to say that, wherever left to the dictation of private landlords, they are, in reference to the greatest happiness of the greatest number, not more various than grievous, resulting indeed in little else than variety of wretchedness.

In order rightly to understand the existing agrarian arrangements, it is almost indispensable to dive pretty deeply into the antiquities of the subject, and if, with the help of the invaluable light afforded by Von Maurer, Nasse, Von Haxthausen, and, above all, so far at least as the present writer is concerned, by Sir Henry Maine, we endeavour to begin at the very beginning, we shall arrive at a time when society consisted of one isolated family, presided over by a father or other ancestor, who ruled with absolute sway, and received unquestioning obedience from subjects trained from their birth in habits of filial submission to their patriarchal superior. Such a family can scarcely be conceived otherwise than as nomad, nor, unless imagined to be still partially dependent for subsistence on the chase, as possessing any wealth other than pastoral. This wealth might theoretically be the joint property of the whole family, but practically it would be entirely at the disposal of the patriarch by whom it was administered, and who, though administering it with a view to the general good, would nevertheless administer it absolutely according to his own discretion. During his lifetime no portion would be severed from the rest without his consent—a consent unlikely to be given except when a female, marrying into another family, received a dower, or when a male, formally emancipated, was permitted to found a separate and independent family, as happened

> What time Dan Abram left the Chaldee land,
> And pastured on from verdant stage to stage,
> Where fields and fountains fresh could best engage.

On the death of the first ancestor, and the consequent devolution of the patriarchate on his eldest son or on some other selected agnate, further severances of the common property might take place. If any of the new patriarch's married brothers, cousins, or nephews, asserted the right of independent control over their respective wives and children, he might find it impossible to resist their claims, or to withhold from them assignments of the general patrimony adequate to the maintenance of their several households. The emancipated relatives, however, would not necessarily remove to a distance, but would usually continue to dwell in the same camp, and to feed their flocks and herds in the same neighbourhood as before; and thus the original single family would gradually expand into a tribe or clan composed of many families, each in its internal affairs governed despotically by a paternal head, but all, in regard to their relations with each other, subject to the control of a council of heads of families, over which the representative, real or assumed, of the first patriarch would probably preside.

We need not linger on the steps by which, from a pastoral tribe thus constituted, might from time to time be thrown off shoots destined to become distinct tribes, and by which a combination of these tribes, and perhaps also of others of different blood, either subjected by force or brought amicably into alliance, might eventually grow into a great pastoral horde or nation. A stage of progress, however, which does somewhat particularly concern us, is that at which a community, whether large or small, from having previously been exclusively pastoral, becomes partially agricultural. A variety of causes may contribute to bring about this change, but the one most frequently and powerfully operative is probably the growth of population, first by narrowing the limits within which a tribe is at liberty to roam, and then by demanding a larger quantity of food than the narrowed range can afford in the form of meat or milk. When the 'substance,' ovine and bovine, and with it the human retinues of Abraham and Lot, increased to an extent threatening hostile collision between their respective herdsmen, the two cousins agreed for peace' sake to halve between them the grazing ground which had previously been common to both, Abraham taking the western and Lot the eastern moiety. Thereupon, Lot is described as at once ceasing to be a wanderer, and as taking up his abode in one of the cities of the plain, while Abraham too, although continuing to dwell in tents, seems to have had them permanently pitched at Mamre, where he presently appears to have added the profession of husbandman to that of herdsman ; for the three measures of fine meal which he bade Sarah knead and make into cakes on the hearth for the stranger guests whom he had, while sitting at the door of his tent, invited to supper, were presumably not less the produce of his own fields than the calf and milk which formed the staple of the feast. At any rate, the urban or village community into which Lot had been admitted by some species of adoption was doubtless semi-agricultural, and into a similar semi-agricultural society the family of Abraham would have expanded at Mamre, if it had remained there long enough for the purpose. If now we proceed to enquire into the nature and constitution of such a society, we are no longer entirely dependent on mere conjectural speculation. We might, indeed, reasonably assume that the community would long preserve unimpaired its collective hold upon the land, and we might conjecture that it would not improbably effect a quadripartite arrangement thereof, covering one portion with homesteads, devoting a second portion to arable or spade husbandry, reserving a third as meadow, and letting the residue remain as waste or forest until a necessity for taking it too into culture should arise. But we need not simply assume this ; we positively know it to be what really occurred. We know that the earliest 'Teutonic cultivating community, as it existed in Germany itself, consisted of a number of families standing in a proprietary relation to a district divided into three' (or four) 'parts. These portions were the *mark* of the township or village, the common mark or waste, and the arable mark or cultivated area,'[1] the latter consisting of two subdivisions, meadow land and land under tillage. We know that similar usages prevailed among the Scandinavian, Sclavonian, and Hindoo branches of the Aryan stock ; they still subsist in full vigour throughout European Russia, and there is no European country in which traces of them do not linger. Even in England, where the peculiarly stringent feudalization of a later period might have been expected to obliterate such footprints of the past, vestiges of the same system are still distinctly observable in the 'common,' 'commonable' or 'open' arable fields, the 'lot meadows' and 'lammas lands' so frequently met with in the Midland and Eastern Counties and also in Surrey, Wiltshire, and Yorkshire, as likewise they are in certain parts of Scotland.[2]

Nor is this all. We know further that 'the community which inhabited the village, held the common mark in mixed ownership, and cultivated the arable mark in lots appropriated to the several families.'[3] The appropriation here referred to is not, however, to be supposed to have

[1] Village Communities in the East and West, by Sir Henry Maine, p. 78.

[2] The system referred to is by no means peculiar to Aryan races. Its close counterpart was found by the old Spanish conquerors flourishing in Mexico and Peru ; and striking resemblances to it may be studied among the Arabs and Kabyles of Algeria, among the negroes of the Gold Coast, and among certain Afghan tribes ; while, as M. De Laveleye has lately pointed out, it may be seen in the Island of Java in a state of organization as complete as, and strikingly resembling, that of Russia. See M. De Laveleye on *La Propriété et ses Formes Primitives*, chaps. iv. and vi.

[3] Maine's Village Communities, p. 78.

been an original feature of the system. While the community was still exclusively pastoral, every one of its component families had possessed and exercised as much right as any other of pasturing its cattle or sheep on any particular portion of the common domain; and for each or for any family to acquire perpetually exclusive rights of tillage over some specified portion would have been a transition much too violently opposed to the general feeling to be allowed to take place immediately after the society became agricultural. It was an easier and more natural gradation to begin with joint tillage of land still regarded as joint property, and many societies still exist which have never advanced beyond this first step in the process. 'In Servia, Croatia, and Austrian Sclavonia, the villages are brotherhoods who are at once co-owners and kinsmen, but the substance of the common property is in their case neither divided in practice nor considered in theory as divisible; the entire land is cultivated by the combined labour of all the villagers, and the produce is annually distributed among the households, sometimes according to their supposed wants, sometimes according to rules which give to particular persons a fixed share of the usufruct.'[1] The same practice was, in the early part of the present century, still followed in the *colonies agricoles* of Auvergne and the Nivernois—of which I have elsewhere[2] given some account—where 'all worked together so far as the nature of their several occupations would permit, were lodged and boarded together, ate at the

[1] Maine's Ancient Law, p. 268.

[2] On Labour, 2nd edition, pp. 487–90.

same table, dressed in the same style, and did all at the general expense; for everything belonged to everybody: all property remained in masses, no one inherited, no one bequeathed; nothing, save means of immediate subsistence, was divided.' And M. De Laveleye, in his interesting work on La Proprieté, has collected several extant examples equally in point, of divers races in all parts of the world whose agriculture still retains one point in common with that of the pre-Jovian age when

> Ne signare quidem aut partiri limite campum
> Fas erat: in medium quærebant.

It will, however, be readily understood that so crude a species of socialism, appealing to no higher feeling than

> Yearnings
> For equal division of unequal earnings,

would, in general, fall after a while into desuetude, and be replaced by arrangements calculated to secure to each family all the fruits of its industry, skill, and thrift, without deduction for the benefit of lazy and improvident members of the community. Among Teutonic races, the following was the expedient adopted with this view. The arable mark proper of each village community appears almost invariably to have been divided into three great fields, in which a rude rotation of crops was enforced, one of the three being left fallow once in three years. To every householder was assigned a family lot in each of the three fields, to be cultivated with his own labour and that of his children and other dependents. Sir Henry Maine conjectures that the distribution thus effected was originally into exactly equal portions, corresponding to the number of free families in the township, but this I am inclined to doubt. Even while the community was still purely pastoral, its component families must have varied a good deal both in numerical strength and in wealth. On becoming agricultural, one of the larger families would perform a proportionably larger share of the common work, and would cover a larger portion of the common land with its operations, and when the common land was divided, might reasonably demand, and could not reasonably be denied, a proportionably larger share for its maintenance, and in order to have sufficient room to work in. But, although, for this reason, there may, from the first, have been considerable inequality of distribution, the tradition of one sort of proprietary equality, that, viz. of equal claim to an assignment in any particular quarter of the common domain, long survived and was kept in life by periodical redistribution of the several assignments. Of such ancient periodical redistribution traces remain, not only in all Teuton or Teutonized countries, but also in almost every country inhabited by an Aryan race. In England, for instance, much of the land, whether arable or meadow, still styled common, has passed into a state of severalty, and is shared among specified bodies of owners. The arable 'common fields are almost invariably divided into three long strips, separated by green baulks of turf; and the several properties consist in subdivisions of these strips, sometimes exceedingly minute, and there is a great deal of evidence that one several share in each of the strips belonged originally to the same ownership.' Even in these arable fields, 'the several shares sometimes, though very rarely, shift from one owner to another in each successive year; but this is frequently the rule with the meadows, which, when in a state of severalty, are often distributed once a year by casting lots amongst the persons entitled to appropriate and enclose them, or else change from one possessor to another in the order of the persons or tenements on a roll.'[1] Similarly, within the bounds of the royalty of the burgh of Lauder, all rights over the common are apparently monopolized by the owners of 105 so-called 'burgess acres,' who periodically distribute a portion of the common amongst them. Of the 1,700 acres of which it consists, about 130 acres are let off once in five or seven years, and an assignment thereof is made over to the owner of each burgess acre, to be broken up and ploughed during that time, at the end of which the 130 acres are again laid down in grass, and another portion of the common is in the same way broken up and ploughed, and again subsequently laid down in grass.[2] Sir Henry Maine, from whom these details are borrowed, reminds the readers of the 'Pirate' of what Scott says of the udal tenures of Orkney and Shetland, and he may himself possibly be glad to be reminded that Waverley, on his way through the hamlet of Tullyveolan to the Baron of Bradwardine's mansion, passed by a 'common field, where the joint labour of the villagers cultivated alternate ridges and patches of rye,

[1] Maine's Village Communities, pp. 85, 86.
[2] Ibid, pp. 95, 96.

oats, barley, and peas, each of such minute extent that, at a little distance, the unprofitable variety of the surface resembled a tailor's book of patterns.' Neither may it be amiss to mention that in the days of 'Auld Wat of Harden,' one of Sir Walter's ancestors, the oxen of laird and feuers all grazed in common. It was shame at hearing the *village herd*, when driving the cattle to pasture, call out loudly for Harden's cow, that made the old chief exclaim '"Harden's cow!" is it come to that pass? By my faith, they shall soon say "Harden's kye;"' and, like the sight of the clean spurs which his wife, the Flower of Yarrow, was wont to place on the table when meat was wanting, urged him to a fresh foraging expedition across the border, whence he returned next day with a bow of kye and a bassened bull.[1]

And this, which is of only exceptional occurrence in Teutonic countries, is still the rule in those inhabited by Sclavonic nations. Recent researches have shown that Russian villages are neither fortuitous congregations of men nor unions founded on contract, but naturally organized communities composed of coheirs whose property is blended, but whose separate rights to distinct proportions of the common domain have become completely recognized. 'The severance of rights, however, in a Russian village, although theoretically complete, is only temporary. After the expiration of a given, but not, in all cases, the same period, separate ownerships are extinguished, the land of the village is thrown into a mass,

[1] Lockhart's Life of Scott, vol. i. p. 93.

and is then redistributed among the families composing the community according to their number. This re-partition having been effected, the rights of families and of individuals are again allowed to branch out into their various lines, which they continue to follow until another period of division comes round.'[1] Very nearly the same language will serve equally well for the Island of Java, the almost complete identity of whose village organization with that of Russia is truly astonishing, and it requires very little modification in order to become applicable likewise to many other remote and widely-separated corners of the globe. Among countries of Aryan occupation, however, it is the Sclavonic alone in which the rule of periodical partition is generally in force. In all the others, the feelings which, after a while, caused what had originally been a common domain cultivated in common to be periodically divided, seem to have continued to operate, and to have occasioned further and most important advances in the transition from collective to individual property. The several families becoming attached to the special lots which they during a series of years had respectively occupied and improved, and becoming unwilling to exchange them for others, may have readily agreed that each should remain in the permanent possession of its assignee. In this way shifting severalties came to an end, and tenements for terms of years became tenements in perpetuity—became, in short, *allods* belonging absolutely to the several families com-

[1] Maine's Ancient Law, pp. 266–67.

posing the community. Yet, although thus rendered essentially allodial, the tenancy of land still retained distinct traces of its old communal character. Every proprietor was bound to observe the same rotation of crops and to practise in certain other particulars the same sort of cultivation as his neighbours. He had still to take a fair share of all communal obligations; and, in the event of his dying without heirs, his property reverted to the community.

It may be asserted with some confidence that, wherever civilized society has been evolved spontaneously and naturally from barbaric germs, the course it has taken has invariably been in all essential respects similar to the one here indicated. That such has been the case in India is scarcely to be disputed, for there the land is still everywhere overspread by village communities in almost every stage of maturity and decay; and it is noteworthy that the least disintegrated specimens of village organization are to be found among the non-Aryan sections of the population. Among the aboriginal peasantry of the Central Provinces there are still occasional examples of the removal of the entire arable mark from one part of the village domain to another, and of the periodical redistribution of lots within the cultivated area, but Sir Henry Maine observes that he has been unable to obtain information of any systematic removal, and still less of any periodical repartition, of the cultivated lands when the cultivators are of Aryan origin.[1] Equally, however, among Aryans and non-Aryans, among Hindoos

[1] Village Communities, p. 112.

and aborigines, subsists a quadripartite arrangement of the communal territory, corresponding exactly with the old Teutonic or Sclavonic mode. 'There is the village consisting of habitations each ruled by a despotic paterfamilias. There is the arable mark, divided into separate lots, but cultivated according to minute customary rules binding on all. Wherever the climate admits of the finer grass crops, there are the reserved meadows, lying generally on the verge of the arable mark. There is the waste or common land, out of which the arable land has been cut, enjoyed as pasture by all the community *pro indiviso*. There too is constantly a council of government to decide disputes as to custom.'[1] But, as already intimated, the village system exhibits very different degrees of vigour in different parts of India. In the north-west and south, where it retains most of its pristine character, the villages are very numerous in which the constitution is decidedly democratic, the chief internal authority being vested in an elected council neither claiming to be nor regarded as being anything more than a representation of the entire cultivating body; but there are also very many villages in which the chief authority has passed to some particular family or families. 'Sometimes the office of headman belongs absolutely to the head of one particular family; sometimes, although it belongs to him primarily, he may be set aside for incapacity or physical blemish; sometimes there is a power of choosing him limited to an election between the

[1] Village Communities, p. 107-8.

members of one or more privileged households.'[1] In Bengal, on the other hand, the system has fallen greatly into decay, and the rights of individual families have acquired a force which has left comparatively little efficacy to the ancient communal bond Throughout India, indeed, the old family assignments are now generally held in perpetuity, and have become converted into properties which are, in their chief essentials, allods, though their allodial character is materially qualified by certain reversionary rights appertaining to the community, and by the obligation of the owners to conform to certain communal rules of culture and to bear their share of certain communal burdens. Here, however, it is important to point out that the Indian village system, although of immemorial antiquity, dating far back into a pre-historic age, and although it has firmly maintained itself while conquest after conquest and revolution after revolution have swept over it, has always, since the very earliest period to which it can be traced, been abjectly subordinate to extrinsic domination. Even in the days of Menu, a Hindoo monarch seems to have been legally entitled to an indefinite, or at all events very ill-defined, share of the gross produce of all the land within his jurisdiction; and, under the subsequent Mahometan sway, the proprietary rights of village communities, though practically tolerated, were theoretically ignored by the doctrine that all the soil belongs in absolute property to the sovereign, and that private property in

[1] Village Communities, p. 155.

land exists only by his sufferance. All 'Indian monarchs of whose practices we have any real knowledge took so much of the produce in the shape of land revenue as to leave to the cultivating groups little more than the means of bare subsistence.'[1] But what they did leave, the village communities were left at liberty to distribute among their respective members according to their own discretion; though, as the possession of such liberty was a matter of little interest except to those communities, it may not improbably have escaped the cognizance of the sovereign.

Such, in outline, was the agrarian system which offered itself to the view of the English on their first becoming dominant in India, but which the new rulers saw only through a glass darkly and with a thick veil of prejudice, legal and other, before their eyes. They were quick enough to apprehend that they had succeeded to the same complete ownership of the soil as had been arrogated by their immediate predecessors, but they were slow to discover that Mahometan despotism had tolerated, consciously or unconsciously, the co-existence of certain private proprietary rights; or if they had any inkling of this, they at any rate failed to perceive that the proprietary unit was not the individual but the family, and that the unit assessable for land taxation was neither the individual nor the family, but the village community. Yet for them, with their strong national prepossessions, the apparent absence of private proprietorship was a painful blank

[1] Village Communities, p. 179.

which they were eager to fill up, and which, in their opinion, could not be suitably filled up except by institutions similar to those with which they had been familiar in their native land. A landlord class seemed to them indispensable for anything like satisfactory social construction, and they looked anxiously round for a class of persons entitled to be so regarded, or capable of being so constituted.

It unfortunately happened that the first considerable provinces which came under British administration were those of Bengal and Behar, where the old village system was more broken up than anywhere else. The village community had there lost much of its primitive cohesiveness, the governing council of elders had disappeared, and though there were still a headman and an accountant, these were no longer elected by the villagers, but were appointed by the State : little, in short, remained to suggest that the community was anything more than a fortuitous assemblage of individuals. At the same time the two provinces had become divided, for fiscal purposes, into a number of districts of very various sizes, each superintended by a zemindar, whose duty it was to collect and account for the land revenue within his jurisdiction, and whose remuneration consisted of a fixed proportion, usually one-eleventh, of the gross receipts. Some of these officers were native princes, representatives of ancient dynasties, which, though reduced to subjection by superior potentates, had never sunk below the condition of tributary rajahs, and had always retained the management of their ancestral domains. Others were the descendants of recent military leaders or robber chiefs, who had begun by levying black mail on their own account, but eventually had come to terms with the Government, and had obtained the management of extensive tracts on condition of paying tribute. Most, however, did not pretend to a higher origin or dignity than that of purely fiscal functionaries, who had in the first instance been appointed to collect and account for the governmental dues, but who, in many cases, profiting by the weakness of the Government of which they held, had ceased to render an account, and had been tacitly permitted to compound by paying whatever amounts had acquired the sanction of custom. Others again may perhaps have corresponded closely to the farmers-general of the French *ancien régime*, and have obtained their positions by regular bargain with the Government, paying stipulated amounts into the treasury, and keeping to themselves whatever surplus they could screw out of the peasantry. But, however different the modes in which the different kinds of zemindars came into being, in one important particular they all closely resembled each other. Conformably to the tendency common at that time to all Indian institutions—a tendency powerfully promoted by the maxim of Hindoo law that a son becomes, by the mere fact and from the moment of his birth, a partner in all property that has descended to his father by inheritance—the zemindary office had come to be regarded as hereditary; and the British authorities, consequently, when looking everywhere around for something akin to perpetual landed proprietorship, fancied that they had discovered among the zemindars some approach to what they sought. Etymology probably contributed to their mystification in the matter, for 'zemindar' in the original Persian means literally 'landholder,' and the name too had by the Moguls been used to distinguish their semi-independent Rajpoot feudatories and other genuine territorial magnates, and thus it the more easily happened that the official personages subsequently known by the same title in Bengal were selected by the British as the foremost parties with whom to conclude the agreement so notorious now as the Permanent Settlement of 1793. From mere revenue officers they were by a stroke of the pen converted into perpetual lessees. The whole country was divided amongst them, to be held at fixed rents, rents fixed for ever at ten-elevenths of the amount which they were supposed to have been in the habit of exacting from the occupants of the cultivated area, while the whole of the waste lands were handed over to them in absolutely and perpetually rent-free ownership. The property thus created was at the same time rendered freely transferable by sale, and it was provided that, on failure by any zemindar to pay the reserved rent of Government as soon as it became due, his estate might be put up to auction and knocked down to the highest bidder with a clear and complete title against all comers. On the other hand, equal power of summary sale was vested in the zemindars for their security against their defaulting sub-tenants.

This Permanent Settlement has passed, and most deservedly, into 'a proverb of maladroit management,'[1]

[1] Village Communities, p. 105.

but, as has been clearly shown by Sir George Campbell, its grand defects are not so much vices of the original conception as results of the negligence with which this was suffered to be carried into effect. It was indeed a heinous sin against posterity gratuitously to aggrandize a number of private individuals by surrendering, utterly and irrecoverably, the undisputed and indisputable right of the State to dispose at its discretion of all future unearned increment of the value of the soil. It was a flagrant robbery of contemporaries to invest the same lucky persons with the proprietorship of the waste lands, for neither in Bengal nor scarcely anywhere else in India, was there any unappropriated land that could equitably be so transferred—wherever the territory of one Indian village terminated that of another commencing, any waste within the limits of either being left waste only until it should be required for cultivation, and being meantime, moreover, partially utilized by the villagers as common pasture, or as common forest for the supply of timber and firewood. Finally, it was, to say the least of it, a recklessly cruel innovation to declare the lands of defaulting sub-holders summarily saleable, in a country where eviction had until then been utterly unheard of. But, bad as these things were, still worse followed, for which it would be the height of injustice to assign the chief responsibility to the legislators of 1793, whose share in the blame thereto attaching is due, not to their failure to issue proper ordinances, but to their neglect to see that those ordinances were properly executed.

In precisely the same manner as the great zemindars

had established and consolidated themselves, inferiors of the same description had grown up under them—sub-chiefs of the original rajah or original robber chief, sub-collectors, and sub-contractors—the positions of whom had, like those of their principals, become hereditary. Under all these again were village headmen, and lower still, the great body of the peasantry in possession of prescriptive rights of occupancy derived from the extinct village associations in which their ancestors had been enrolled. It is commonly supposed that in the settlement of 1793 the rights and claims of these sub-holders were overlooked and confiscated, and that to their absolute exclusion the zemindars were constituted complete and sole proprietors. The real truth is diametrically the reverse of this. As between the Government and the zemindars, the claims of the former were strictly limited, so with not less distinctness were those of the zemindars in regard to all below them. Subholders of territorial subdivisions were assured of their tenancies conditionally on payment of their regulated dues, while with respect to the ryots or peasants it was ordained that the rent payable by each should be specified in writing, any dispute as to the amount being determined by the civil court of the district according to the usage of the neighbourhood respecting lands of the same description and quality as those in question; and it was further provided that the ryots should always be entitled to renewed leases at rents determined on the same principles as those of the recorded rents. In short, as far as the letter of the law went, fixity of tenure at specified rates was assured to all concerned, but unfortunately the portion of the law applicable to the peasantry was never enforced. No record of the rights of the ryots was ever made, and in its absence any complaints of, or claims to, increase of rent which came into court were disposed of in accordance with English ideas; legislative decrees were overridden by judicial decisions; and thus, by a rapid prescriptive process, the zemindars of Bengal became what we now see them, close counterparts, that is, not so much of English as of Irish landlords, practically at liberty to extort whatever the ryots can, by threats of eviction or otherwise, be induced to pay. For a considerable time they seem not to have greatly abused their licence of exaction, and to have remained content with continually demanding small additions to the accustomed rents. Indolence, acting as a salutary check upon rapacity, persuaded them to accept quietly what they could easily get rather than bestir themselves painfully to get more, which, moreover, they were the less disposed to do, because they were somewhat tardy in fully appreciating the prerogatives of occidental proprietorship. On this head, however, the numerous European indigo planters who have gradually become intermixed with them, have of late years greatly enlightened them both by precept and example; and it is clear from the evidence of Colonel Haig, with which this chapter commenced, and from further evidence presently to be adduced, that they have no intention of hiding their new light under a bushel.

A policy known by such fruits might perhaps retain a large band of ardent partizans in the land of its nativity, but was scarcely likely to be viewed with much admiration elsewhere; and in the Madras territories, the theatre of the next great agrarian experiment, the Government rushed into a directly opposite extreme. One capital vice was borrowed from Bengal. The sin against posterity, involved in abandonment of the State's share of all future increase in the soil's value, was repeated in a modified form, but this was the sole point of resemblance between the two systems. In the south, zemiṇdars, lùmberdars, polygars, *et hoc genus omne*, were for the most part ignored, and the parties selected to be directly dealt with were the individual ryots or cultivating tenants, each of whom was separately assessed for the land held by him, and was assured of its possession so long as he should continue to pay the revenue assessed. The tenure resulting from this 'ryotwar' settlement, as it is officially termed, is often spoken of as peasant proprietorship, but seldom has so honourable an appellation been more unworthily bestowed. The distinctive excellence of every tenure really deserving to be so designated is the stimulus it gives to industry, skill and thrift, by making all increase of produce resulting from exhibition of those qualities, the reward of him by whom they are exhibited. But if it had been the set purpose of the Madras authorities to prevent such stimulus from being applied, they could scarcely have gone to work more perversely. A maximum was indeed fixed which the Government assessment was never to exceed, but it was fixed at a point greatly above what could, in the then existing state of agriculture and with the prices then current, be ordinarily paid. Practically, whatever was the actual assessment of one year, it was liable to be raised in the next, nor was the liability by any means permitted to lie dormant. If a ryot dug a well in order to water his fields, or accepted water from a neighbouring tank or canal, his rent might not improbably be doubled on account of the change from dry to wet cultivation. If, in order to get more out of the land, he grew two successive crops in the same year, he was charged double instead of single crop rates, and he incurred a similar penalty if he substituted a more valuable for a less valuable crop, being charged perhaps three rupees an acre while growing millet, and eighteen when changing to tobacco. By expedients like these he was continually given to understand that the one sure consequence of improved husbandry on his part would be his subjection to increased exaction. True, as long as he continued to pay the rent customary in his vicinity he could not be, or at least never was, evicted, but his hold upon the land, nevertheless, was much more akin to rack-rented tenancy at will than to any species of beneficial ownership. I am speaking, it will be understood, of the Madras system as it was originally framed, and before it had received some recent amendments by which some of its worst defects have been partially remedied. It was established during the Governorship of Sir Thomas Munro, which ceased in 1827, and in 1869 its results were thus summed up in an official report addressed to the Madras Board of Revenue:—'The bulk of the people are paupers. They can just pay their cess in a good year, and fail altogether when the season is bad. Remissions have to be made perhaps every year in most districts, and there is a bad season in some one district or group of districts every year.'[1]

As in the Madras territories, so likewise in those of the Bombay Presidency, the prevailing settlement is ryotwaree, but it is one of a far better pattern. There, too, the cultivating occupants are dealt with directly and individually, but the grand mistakes of perpetual limitation of the public demand on the one hand, and of excessively heavy immediate demands on the other, have been carefully avoided, and the medium course has been adopted of charging very low—perhaps too low—rates, and declaring them unchangeable for thirty years, though liable to enhancement at the end of that period. The Bombay ryots are not much better entitled than their brethren of Madras to be styled peasant proprietors; but if the settle-

[1] Cobden Club Volume on Systems of Land Tenure, p. 201. The account given in the text does not pretend to exhibit more than the principal outlines of the several Indian revenue systems, and would require material corrections in order to be rendered strictly accurate even in regard to these. Considerable portions of the Bengal territories, for instance, have never been included within the permanent settlement; while in the Madras Presidency, on the other hand, although the prevailing settlement be ryotwaree, there are three provinces in which perpetual arrangements after the Bengal fashion were at an early period made with zemindars. But it would seem to be beyond the capacity of any but local adepts of lifelong training faithfully to describe Madras revenue affairs, which, says Sir George Campbell, 'have always been a kind of sacred mystery to the outside world, so full are the reports concerning them of native complications, and so bristling with hopelessly unintelligible complications. Even I,' he adds, 'an expert of many provinces, shrink from them. An ordinary Englishman might as well attempt to read an arrow-headed inscription.'—Cobden Club Volume on Systems of Land Tenure, p. 199.

ment with them be periodically renewed on the same moderate principles as those on which it was originally based, they will occupy the next best position, that, viz. of perpetual lessees, at an always equally light though not stationary rent. So far as it has hitherto proceeded, the Bombay plan is admitted on all hands to have worked admirably. It is extremely popular with the tenantry, and the proprietary Government has every reason to be satisfied with it. The first period of thirty years expired some time ago, and several districts have been re-settled. In one of these, that of Bhimturi, in the collectorate of Poona, the people were, in 1841, in an abject state of poverty and wretchedness. In 1871, the population had increased 39½ per cent.; the number of carts from 273 to 1,011; the number of ploughs 22½ per cent., and that of bullocks 19 per cent. In 1840, there were 527 wells in working order—now there are 727; and the whole cultivable area is taken up. 'In the Chandur district, belonging to the collectorate of Nassick, population since 1840 has increased 100 per cent.; the number of carts from 903 to 2,747; of bullocks from 8,602 to 13,988; of wells from 712 to 1,076. In 1840, the number of acres under cultivation was 95,867; it is now 110,223, and the new settlement increases the land revenue by 52 per cent.' These districts 'may be taken as samples of many others.' [1]

Until about twenty years ago, the north-westerly portion of Anglo-India consisted of the territories, other

[1] Markham's Statement of Moral and Material Progress of India for 1872-73, p. 27.

than the kingdom of Oude, intermediate between Behar and the River Jumna, and the same territories, notwithstanding the subsequent acquisition of some of the Cis-Sutlej States and of the Punjab, are still officially styled the North-Western Provinces. These came into our possession early in the present century, but it was not until 1822 that any steps were taken towards a general settlement of the land revenue, nor, for a whole decade thereafter, were many of the steps taken other than preliminary. During the next ten years, however, settlement operations were carried on vigorously, but the principles on which they proceeded were, with one signal exception, essentially the same, although no doubt very materially mitigated, as those which had vitiated analogous operations in Bengal. The worse than blunder, the criminal folly of sacrificing gratuitously and irrecoverably the right of the State to share in future increments of the value of the soil was not committed; it had apparently ceased to be supposed that because some fixity of tenure is an indispensable element in all good land revenue arrangements, therefore rent ought to be fixed in perpetuity, and the period during which the Government demand was to remain stationary was therefore limited to thirty years. But it was not perceived that the class of persons whose rents it is most desirable temporarily to fix are those who have the strongest motives to improve the land, to wit, the actual cultivators. The English superstition in favour of a rural aristocracy, which, though discredited in the south of India, was as rampant as ever among the pupils of the Cornwallis school, who were now administering the North-West, permitted no direct dealings with individual, nor, unless there were absolutely no alternative, even with associated, ryots. Wherever any persons could be found exercising powers in any degree similar to those of English landlords, they were recognized and aggrandized; wherever they could not be found, they were created. Throughout the North-West, the communal village system still retained much of its early vitality. By the Emperor Akbar, in imitation probably of immemorial usage, the village community had, two centuries previously, been adopted as the assessable unit, but the pretensions of either associated or individual ryots to be so treated were now almost entirely misapprehended and proportionably disregarded. In the interval which had elapsed since Akbar's reign, various functionaries had succeeded in interposing themselves between the Government and the peasantry. There were numerous village headmen, chiefs of provincial families, collectors of, or contractors for, revenue, all claiming to be hereditary, and claiming too a species of suzerainty over single villages or groups of villages, and sometimes over whole districts; and, under the larger of these office-holders, had grown up a body of secondary middlemen, with similar hereditary or semi-hereditary pretensions. With persons of one or other of these classes, wherever any such could be discovered, the British authorities made their arrangements, selecting, where superiors and subordinates had concurrent or conflicting claims, sometimes the former, sometimes the latter—pensioning or otherwise compensating those whom they rejected, and converting the selected, not indeed into absolute landowners, but into what was nearly the same thing, viz. into thirty-years leaseholders at low rents, with a right to renewal at a revaluation on the expiration of the leases. In villages in which neither the headman nor anyone else pretended to any rights over any lands except those in his own occupancy, either the headman or some other respectable villager was nevertheless constituted leaseholder of the entire village on the same terms as those just mentioned.

This important change was accompanied by another of even graver import. From Akbar's time downwards, the whole of the revenue leviable on a village community had been held to be legally the due of the State, although the interception of part of it by the collecting middleman was sanctioned or tolerated. But now it was with the metamorphosed and exalted middleman that the State made its bargain, holding him responsible for a specified sum, and leaving to him whatever surplus might be paid by the cultivators of the soil, inclusive, of course, of whatever addition to present rents might become obtainable in consequence either of extended cultivation or of any other legitimate cause. It is true that the ryots were not formally abandoned to the tender mercies of the newly-created zemindars. On the contrary, not only was it enacted that their customary rights should be carefully investigated, ascertained, and recorded, but what purported to be a complete record of those rights was actually drawn up. Unfortunately, the framing of the record was committed to officers with decided prepossessions in favour of a regularly graduated landed aristocracy, while its subsequent interpretation was left to tribunals equally prejudiced in the same direction. Among the questions at issue, two were especially prominent—one, what length of past occupation carried with it future rights of occupancy, the other, what power of raising the rents of 'occupancy ryots' legally appertained to the zemindars; and to neither question could a decisive answer be obtained by appeal to custom, which, nevertheless, was, in the circumstances of the case, the best, if not the only possible referee. If it was impossible for the zemindars to establish a prescriptive right on their part to irregular exaction, so too was it for the ryots to prove that they had been constantly exempt from such exaction. The first point was, however, disposed of fairly enough by a compromise to the effect that all cultivating ryots, who had been in uninterrupted possession for twelve years, without special contract, should be held to have the right of occupancy; but with regard to the second, the only express provision was that power to realise rent by summary process should apply only to the rent recorded as previously payable; and this restriction was subsequently set aside by decisions given in the civil courts that a zemindar, on showing that causes independent of the exertions of the ryot had raised the value of the land, was entitled to obtain by regular suit an increase of rent.[1] What was thus judicially decreed has since, by Act X. of 1859, been legislatively confirmed and extended, and the North-Western zemin-

[1] Campbell, in Cobden vol., on Systems of Land Tenure, p. 186.

dar now occupies, in relation even to 'occupancy' ryots, almost precisely the same legal position as an English landlord in respect to tenants-at-will. It would seem, however, that as yet the zemindars have not at all generally availed themselves of their enlarged powers, and have for the most part allowed the ryots to remain at unvaried rents; and though it is scarcely to be expected that they will continue to escape the contagion of the example which is beginning to be set by some of their fellows in Bengal, it is meanwhile satisfactory to have the assurance of so unimpeachable a witness as Sir George Campbell, that the operation of the North-Western settlement has so far been in the main good, that a great impulse has been given to agriculture, that the country has flourished in peace and prosperity without other interruption than the signal one of the Sepoy mutiny, that land has greatly risen in value, and that from these manifold advantages the principal drawback is the dispossession by legal process and the consequent political alienation of very many improvident and insolvent members of the newly-constituted zemindars.

The settlement of the Punjab, a geographical expression recently so extended as to comprehend not only the country of the 'Five Rivers'—the Indus and its affluents—but also the Cis-Sutlej territories as far as Delhi inclusive, was effected under the auspices and during the Commissionership of the present Lord Lawrence, and is an immense improvement on that of the so-called North-Western Provinces. It partakes largely of the ryotwarree character, and may indeed be described as essentially ryotwarree with a wholesome intermixture of extraneous characteristics. The assessment is moderate—only one-half of the rent which had customarily been paid, or was held to be customarily payable by the cultivators—and it was fixed for a period of thirty years, but arrangements were in most instances made, not with quasi-proprietary individuals, whether of prescriptive growth or of new creation, but with the village communities, which in the Punjab proper and in the country immediately to the eastward, have retained, in a measure unusual elsewhere, their original internal cohesiveness. Each community is collectively responsible for the amount at which it is assessed, which amount is levied, by a representative council of elders, upon the individual members, in proportions corresponding with the portions of land which they respectively occupy. Of course, the several villagers are in turn individually responsible to the village council, which may by sale or otherwise, temporarily or in perpetuity, transfer a defaulter's fields to a solvent tenant; but feelings of civic fellowship render measures of such harshness extremely rare, and a reciprocal sense of civic duty prevents occasions for them from often arising. Even in cases in which they can no longer be altogether avoided, some person is generally found ready to take charge of the defaulter's tenement in a quality analogous to that of mortgagee, discharging its pecuniary obligations and appropriating the surplus profits, until the temporarily ousted owner returns with the means of making the compensation requisite for the redemption of his property. Under conditions like these, abundant inducement to agricultural improvement is afforded by the plenary interest in its fruits vested in the improver during a long series of years, at the end of which the Government recovers its right to participate in the increase of annual wealth which its own politic liberality has called into existence. Possibly its liberality during the interval may have been somewhat excessive—possibly its demand during the first thirty years may have been needlessly low—but even so, it is still the great body of the peasantry, and not arbitrarily selected individuals, who have benefited directly, while Government has its reward indirectly in the material well-being and political content of the rural population. This has already on one memorable occasion rendered genuine yeoman service.

The land settlement was scarcely yet complete when the Sepoy mutiny of 1857 afforded to a warlike, high-spirited, and recently-subjugated people, a grand opportunity of recovering their independence. But Lord Lawrence's enlightened policy had already converted the natural animosity of the country people into hearty and active loyalty. The Punjabees not only did not rebel, but co-operated most efficaciously in putting down rebellion. With arms placed in their hands by their foreign masters, the villagers fought against the mutineers, hunted down the fugitives, and, enrolled by thousands in hastily-organised regiments, contributed largely to the recapture of Delhi. Right well earned was the praise obtained by Lord Lawrence of having preserved India for his countrymen in that tremendous emergency, but it was earned less by what he did at the time, than by what he had done before. His fertility of resource, his unflinching intrepidity, his readiness of conception, and rapidity of execution, would have availed little, if the beneficence of his previous administration had not furnished him with abundance of willing instruments, by transforming into grateful friends those who might otherwise have proved most formidable and implacable enemies.

The land settlement of Oude, which was commenced in 1856, immediately after incorporation of that kingdom with the British dominions, very strikingly illustrates the vacillation and fickleness of purpose which are the bane of Anglo-Indian statesmanship. Under the feeble sway of the deposed dynasty, numerous talookdars, a term synonymous in Oude with that of zemindars in Bengal, had, by usurpation or prescription, or both, acquired a quasi-proprietary hold on two-thirds of the soil, but their claims on this account were in the first instance summarily set aside by their new rulers, or at best reserved for subsequent investigation, and all revenue arrangements were meantime made directly with the village communities. In the following year, 1857, the mutiny broke out, and not only did the dispossessed talookdars at once join eagerly in the insurrection, but so likewise did the ryots, who had long been attached to the talookdars by feudal ties, and apparently, too, by not a little of genuine feudal affection, and who had not yet had time to appreciate the value of the new privileges just conferred on themselves. This opened the eyes of Government to the injustice it had unwittingly committed, and a violent reaction thereupon took place. Although in 1858, after the suppression of the rebellion, Lord Canning, as Viceroy, issued his famous proclamation formally confiscating all the lands in Oude, he did so merely in order to re-grant them immediately afterwards to the talookdars with titles far more complete and absolute than they had ever previously pretended to. Their semi-proprietary character was not only legally recognized but recognized in perpetuity, and settlements were made with them for periods of twenty or thirty years, during which the gross rental was to be equally divided between themselves and the Government; while they were, moreover, given to understand that similar proportions would be observed in all subsequent settlements. So far the Government had been acting, however recklessly, strictly within its competence, but, in its further proceedings, it showed itself as lavish of the rights of others as it had already been of its own. Lord Canning did indeed stipulate on behalf of the ryots that any subordinate rights of theirs which could be proved to have been in active existence at the date of annexation should be maintained, but, to the settlement officers on whom it devolved to judge of the sufficiency of proof, and who were for the most part strongly tinged with anti-ryotwar prejudices, very considerable latitude was necessarily allowed. There was no established standard for them to go by; the ryots themselves only hazily conceived that they might possibly possess some right apart from might. Even while most strongly insisting that a talookdar ought not to turn them out, they would, if questioned on the point, admit that he had always possessed the power of turning them out. 'Of course he had,' they would say, 'the man in power can do anything.' Still, if the ryots could seldom prove a right to stay in, as rarely could the talookdars prove a right to turn them out, but, as the settlement officers thought proper to place the burden of proof on the ryots, the latter very generally failed to make good their claim to any legal status, and the final result was that, although a comparatively small number were registered as possessing hereditary rights of occupancy, the great mass were reduced to a position little above that of tenants at will. As I understand the matter, the ryots distinguished as hereditary are not to have their rents raised during the currency of the settlement, nor even at its close without the concurrence of the revenue authorities ; but, to all ryots other than hereditary, no alternative has been left but that of accepting whatever conditions of tenure the talookdars may be disposed to grant. The English territorial system has been by law established in Oude almost in its entirety, with most of its manifold inherent evils, and also with whatever of good may inherently belong to it. Such is the last result of a whole century of experimental study : such the latest achievement of the Anglo-Indian Government in the arena of land-revenue management.

It is in no captious or censorious spirit that, in this necessarily brief sketch of agrarian legislation in different parts of Anglo-India, especial stress has been laid upon the errors committed. The chief use of any historical retrospect consists in the hints it offers for future guidance—a clear perception of the length and direction in which we have hitherto gone wrong being the best security for our henceforth shaping our course aright. In land revenue affairs there are two duties peculiarly incumbent on the State: one, to preserve intact all rights vested in itself as trustee for the public; the other, to watch, protect, and foster the interests of the peasantry, as being at once the most numerous and most defenceless portion of the rural population; and these are precisely the duties on which the British authorities in India have bestowed least attention.

To the economic dogma that all taxation is economically bad, there is one great exception. An immemorial land tax, even though legally susceptible of augmentation to equality with the full rent—to equality, that is, with the balance of produce remaining after deduction of the expenses of cultivation, plus profit at the current rate on the amount of those expenses, is, provided it be not permitted to exceed the full rent, free from all, even the minutest economic objection. The existence of such a tax would imply that the community at large, to which the land must manifestly have at first belonged, did not, while acquiescing in the occupation of portions of the soil, whether temporarily or permanently, by individuals, sanction the establishment of private ownership therein, but, retaining all its own proprietary rights, had continued to be sole and universal landlord. The land tax, whatever, within the limits specified, its amount, would simply be so much reserved rent; and rent, according to the definition just given, leaving as it does to capital the full current rate of profit, evidently imposes not the smallest burthen upon industry. Whatever cultivated land produces, the surplus constituting rent, must inevitably be taken as rent by somebody, and the result to industry is the same, or rather industry remains equally unaffected in both cases, whether the recipients of rent be the State or certain private individuals, unless indeed those individuals be the immediate tenants and cultivators of the soil. Nay, aboriginal appropriation by the State of all or part of the rent proper, under the name of land tax, may afford positive relief to industry by diminishing the necessity for imposition of other and directly anti-industrial taxes. Such appropriation is in fact maligned by being classed as taxation, for it takes nothing from anyone, but is simply assumption, on behalf of the public, of that which has immemorially belonged to the public—of something to which none but the public ever had any just pretension, and which none were ever permitted, even temporarily, to enjoy except by public indulgence. And while the State rent here indicated is not merely economically unexceptionable but economically meritorious, it is, if indefinitely extensible, the most valuable of fiscal resources, for its productiveness must necessarily, unless artificially restrained, increase simultaneously with every augmentation of national wealth. In proportion as the prices of agricultural produce rise in consequence of the people becoming more numerous or richer, the rent of land will increase too, and the State may appropriate for public use the whole or any part of the increment, without depriving any private individuals of anything that has ever been theirs. The revenue so obtained is a fund in whose advantages the whole community participates, but to which none of its members have contributed. Now all Indian Governments prior to our own had this most precious of fiscal resources at command. Everyone of them occupied the position of landlord-general, with rent-levying rights unlimited by law, and limited, if at all, by custom. In the days of Menu, the king might irreproachably take a fourth part of the produce of the soil. During the period of Mahometan sway he took what he pleased—generally perhaps one-third, or two-fifths, but not seldom one-half: his exactions were always arbitrary and uncertain, and often grievously exhaustive. But the utility of power is not disproved by its liability to abuse; a man need not cut off his right hand to disable himself from committing robbery or murder; and when the Anglo-Indian Government succeeded by conquest to the landlord-generalship of Bengal, it might surely have trusted itself to exercise the rights appertaining to that office with whatever moderation appeared to itself meet. It preferred, however, altogether to divest itself of those rights, and accordingly proceeded to cripple itself for ever by a self-denying ordinance almost without parallel for its perverse fatuity. If anyone deem this too vehement a denunciation of Lord Cornwallis's permanent settlement, let him ponder well over one solitary fact. In 1793 the total rental of Bengal, Behar, and Orissa, was rather over 3,400,000*l.*, of which ten-elevenths, or say 3,100,000*l.*, went into the public treasury, the remaining eleventh, or about 300,000*l.* being intercepted by the zemindars. Thanks to the permanent settlement of that year, Government's share is much the same now as it was then, while the share of the zemindars has, according to income tax statistics, risen to between seven and eight millions sterling, nearly the whole of which would, in the ordinary conrse of things, have formed part of the annual income of the State. Truly, to the present Viceroy and his Finance Minister, to Lord Northbrook and Sir William Muir, sadly solicitous how best to re-establish equilibrium between incomings and outgoings, it must be tantalizing to reflect that, but for Lord Cornwallis's interposition, there might be no cause for such melancholy musings—no need to watch so wistfully the varying prospects of the opium market, or anxiously to enquire whether another British regiment or two may not be spared from India's already too weak garrison, or which of her parched and trackless districts may best contrive to get on a little longer without watercourses or roads.

Some comfort there might be if one could only hope that the lesson taught by such costly experience had at length, however tardily, been thoroughly learnt; but, alas! it was so recent a Governor-General as Lord Canning who issued a decree which, if carried into full effect, would eventually have made permanency of settlement universal; and though wiser counsels have since prevailed, still, from time to time, the old cuckoo cry is revived by able editors and eloquent orators, both here and in India, and permanency of settlement is still vaunted as a panacea for all India's social disorders. With such notions still current, it would be premature to let bygones be bygones, and a few minutes may be not unprofitably spent in analysing the process of reasoning which resulted in the grand mistake committed towards the close of the last century, and still in danger of being repeated.

There is land, look you, in Britain, and there is land in Bengal, so equally should there be landlords in both. Such apparently was the logic, parodied from Captain Fluellen's, which was prevalent in high quarters in 1793. Doubtless, from Indian landlords modelled after the British type, the discharge of certain useful functions was expected. Being assured of all profits accruing from any agricultural improvements effected by themselves, they might perceive it to be for their interest to come forward as improvers, to engage in the reclamation of wastes, and to introduce new plants and better processes on lands already under tillage. Civilizing centres too, each in his own circle, they might prove, whence rays of refinement might permeate the atmosphere breathed by the surrounding boors, to whom, moreover, they might act as unpaid magistrates, and by whom the example set by them of grateful loyalty to a beneficent Government might be passively followed. But although fixity of tenure be undoubtedly a necessary condition of progressive husbandry, it does not follow that the fixity need be perpetual, and moreover, whether temporary or permanent, it is the husbandmen immediately occupying the soil upon whom possession of such fixity would act most powerfully stimulative. If between these and the Government, an intermediate squirearchy of spontaneous growth were already in existence, well and good, by all means should its prescriptive privileges have been scrupulously respected: but to create artificially such a class, and to endow it with a large share of the national substance, was surely to pay a most extravagant price for any services, economic, social, or political, which it could possibly render. And to what extent is it that the zemindars of Bengal have answered expectation? Even Sir Henry Maine speaks of them as having 'the worst reputation as landlords,' adding that 'they appear frequently to have deserved it;' and in spite of his habitual calmness inveighs against their 'political worthlessness,' their 'failure to obtain any wholesome influence over the peasantry,' and their 'oppression of all inferior holders.' Some of them have indeed permitted their waste lands to be colonized by adventurous ryots, but bare permission is all the aid which they have afforded to the enterprise. To seek for instances of their having, like the Duke of Sutherland in the county from which that nobleman takes his title, paved the way by making roads, cutting drains, or building cottages, might perhaps be unfair, and would certainly be idle; and equally vain would be a search among them for enthusiastic agricultural amateurs like our Cokes and Townshends, our Pagets, Huxtables, and Conroys. Their pastimes for the most part are decidedly the reverse of edifying, and as ill suited as need be for imitation by an admiring tenantry; while, as for their political gratitude, that shows itself simply as a keen sense of favours to come, and in insolent protests against liability to any new imposts, general or local—to either a tax on income or to road or education cesses. Whoever else may be subject to these, their own claims to exemption in the capacity of permanently assessed landholders, must, they loudly insist, be held inviolate. Such is the return of the rural nobility and gentry of Bengal for the lavish indulgence with which they have been pampered, for the reckless sacrifices made for their behoof, whereof, moreover, that of the national revenue is far from the most important. Whatever abatement Goldsmith's panegyric of a 'bold peasantry' as 'their country's pride' may require, it is nevertheless certain that a country which has no reason to be proud of its peasantry cannot have much ground of any sort for boasting. A great and prosperous nation with a degraded and wretched peasantry is the play of 'Hamlet' with the part of Hamlet left out, and this is especially true of a country where two-thirds of the population are tillers of the ground. Now the well or ill being of the agricultural classes depends mainly on the character of their connection with, and hold upon, the soil. To favour even this portion of the community, prop and stay though it be of the remainder, at the general expense, might be unwise: to endow a peasantry with portions of the national domain, or to curtail the proprietary rights exercised over them by a class above, may be heroic remedies to be resorted to only in the last extremity; but surely, at least, any prescriptive rights appertaining to themselves ought to be held scrupulously sacred. They are about the last persons to whom should be applied the principle of taking from him that hath not even that which he seemeth to have, in order to give to him that hath, so that he may have more abundance. Yet this is precisely what the British authorities have done or suffered to be done in respect to the ryots of Bengal and the adjoining provinces, and that to an extent which is simply scandalous: no gentler phrase will serve the turn. Under native domination mere tenancy-at-will may almost be said to have been unknown. Any families which had been sitting for one or two generations on the same land were usually regarded as entitled to continue to sit at rents bearing the same proportion as before to the gross produce. And the demands made even upon the newest settlers were generally regulated by the custom of the neighbourhood, eviction even in regard to them being a practice almost unheard of. Extortion no doubt was frequent, but it was well understood on both sides to be extortion, and an invasion of rights sanctioned by law written or unwritten.

How, in many instances, these rights of the lowly were, for the sake of further aggrandizing metamorphosed tax-collectors and farmers of revenue, thrown as inconsidered trifles into the scale; how, where not formally confiscated, they have been suffered to perish through neglect, has already been noted, but hardly sufficiently. It seems to be commonly supposed that the proprietary powers created at the expense of the ryots have not on the whole been grossly abused, and that the country gentry of Bengal, although taking as much as they can without trouble squeeze out of the tenantry, seldom exercise any pressure requiring much effort on their part. Recent disclosures, however, show that this statement of the case is not to be accepted without very considerable qualification. Reporting, in the capacity of Lieutenant-Governor, on the Administration of Bengal for 1871–72, Sir George Campbell expressed himself as follows:—'It is too certainly the case that very much larger cesses than are levied for public purposes are habitually levied by zemindars for their own benefit, and in nothing is the distinction between the benefits claimed under the permanent settlement and the way in which the obligations of that settlement are set at naught, more striking than in this respect. The regulation by which the permanent settlement was established rigorously laid down that all payments due by the ryots to the landholders must be included in the one rent, and that no other cesses or exactions of any kind were to be taken by the zemindar on any pretext whatever. It is known that such cesses are nevertheless very generally levied under various forms, in great number, and sometimes to an excessive amount.'[1] In the Report for the following year he adds, that on further enquiry these irregular levies have been found to be 'much larger, more numerous, and more universal than had been at all suspected. Although at the time of the permanent settlement most of such demands were abolished as far as the law could abolish them, and all that remained were amalgamated with the rent, a fresh crop of them has since grown up with a rank luxuriance.' Further on, he describes agricultural cesses as consisting of 'various dues and charges levied from the ryots in addition to the regular rent, and generally in

[1] Page 169.

proportion to the rent. The modern zemindar taxes his ryots for the support of his agents of various kinds and degrees, for the payment of his income tax and his postal cess, for the purchase of an elephant for his own use, for the cost of the stationery of his establishment, for the cost of printing the forms of his rent receipts, for the payment of his lawyers. The milkman gives his milk, the oilman his oil, the weaver his cloth, the confectioner his sweetmeats, the fisherman his fish. The zemindar levies benevolences from his ryots for a festival, for a religious ceremony, for a birth, for a marriage; he exacts fees from them on all changes of their holdings, on the exchange of leases and agreements, and on all transfers and sales; he imposes a fine on them when he settles their petty disputes, and when the police or when the magistrate visit his estates; he levies black mail on them when social scandals transpire, or when an offence or an affray is committed. He establishes his private pound near his counting-house, and realizes a fine for every head of cattle that is caught trespassing on the ryots' crops. It has been the ryots' immemorial practice to pay these *abwabs*, as they are called, and they pay accordingly; they pay because they have always paid, and because in the long run it involves less trouble to pay than to refuse.'[1]

One typical case deserves to be given somewhat in detail. A posse of zemindaree bullies 'proceeded to a small hamlet in Nuddea inhabited by some ten or fifteen

[1] Report for 1872–3, part i. p. 17, and part iii. pp. 23, 26.

householders, neither of substance nor yet of exceptional poverty, and apportioning on an average their requirements at the rate of twopence farthing to every shilling, demanded a benevolence of between two and three pounds. This amount was actually realized, yet the ryots did not complain; they never would have complained had the zemindars allowed matters to stop at this point; but the zemindars ventured, within three or four days afterwards, to impose another cess of four pounds upon the same petty village as its contribution towards the marriage expenses of the daughter of one of their own number. Yet even in these straits the ryots exhausted every means of complying with the additional exaction. They sowed indigo for the planter, and they applied to him for assistance, but in vain; they besought their money-lender for the money, but fruitlessly; and only as a last resource petitioned the magistrate for redress. The case was especially reported upon by the Board of Revenue, who observed "that it seemed to prove the unmerciful manner in which unauthorized cesses are demanded; the fear of the oppressed ryots which induces them to comply with oppressive demands, of the illegality of which they may be aware, and the extreme difficulty of obtaining any adequate redress; and to show conclusively that some means should be afforded by the Government to check the rapacity of the zemindars and their agents, and to afford protection to their victims."'[1]

This is the state of affairs in Bengal proper, but that

[1] Report for 1872-3, pp. 25, 26.

which recent enquiries have brought to light in Orissa is yet more disgraceful—one, says Sir George Campbell, 'which could hardly have been credited, so completely have the rights of the ryots, once well-established and formally recorded, been over-ridden by the superior landholders.' The agrarian arrangements of that province were entirely different from those of Bengal. 'A regular settlement had been made some thirty years ago, whereby the rights of the ryots were not only acknowledged, but ascertained, recorded, and secured by documents issued by Government direct. *But the Bengal Board of Revenue entertained a strong dislike to the old system of public record through village and district accountants*, which has been maintained in other parts of India; and in Orissa, where these indigenous institutions had been in full force, they were suppressed and disused,' so that 'the records made thirty-five years ago have never been continued or kept up. The Government settlement made direct with the hereditary ryots has consequently been utterly set at naught; the Government leases have been taken from the ryots; the rents fixed by the Government officers have been increased many fold; and the main object of the extension of the settlement for a fresh term of thirty years after the famine, viz. that of permitting the ryots to hold on at the old settlement rates, has been utterly defeated.'[1] It is scarcely worth while adding that when remissions of land revenue were granted by Government on account of the famine of 1866, 'on the express condition that the rents of the ryots should also be remitted,

[1] Report for 1872-3, part i. p. 16, and part iii. p. 27.

the zemindars, as a rule, did not give the benefit of either the remissions or the advances they received to the ryots, but continued to collect their rents.'

The sins involved in the revenue settlement of Bengal have, as we have seen, been repeated in Oude, although with diminished heinousness, inasmuch as the right of the State to share in the increased value of the land will, after a certain lapse of time, revive, while the revenue officers will be entitled, and, without inexcusable neglect of duty, cannot fail, to interpose on behalf of certain privileged ryots, and to enforce a fair division of the remaining increment of value in prescribed proportions between them and the talookdars. In the North-West Provinces, the Government, in granting long leases to the superior landholders, has in so far acted the part of an enlightened landlord, though the evil consequences of its neglect to protect the inferior tenants from oppression are likely to become more obvious as time goes on; but it can scarcely be acquitted of culpable improvidence in having, when recently renewing the leases, so greatly reduced its already very moderate demands, that the net land revenue of the North-West Provinces was nearly 400,000*l.* less in 1872 than it had been in 1842, notwithstanding the extension of cultivation and the rise of prices during the interval.

The chief faults of the Madras revenue settlement are of a contrary character. It spares the peasantry the curse of middlemen, but the combined effect of too high a maximum of assessment, and of the liability of the assessment to be continually varied within the limits of the maximum, places the peasantry in a position too nearly akin to that of a rack-rented tenantry.

Still from amidst so many disheartening circumstances, one or two consolations arise. The mischief as yet done is not universal, nor, where most serious, is it altogether unsusceptible of remedy, still less of mitigation. Even in Bengal, notwithstanding the pains perversely there taken to render the evil permanent, opportunities are continually occurring for the application of a curative process, in respect to which, moreover, valuable hints may be derived from the wiser policy pursued in the Bombay territories and the Punjab. The first generation of Bengal zemindars of British manufacture were slow in conforming to the obligation of paying the dues of the State on the day appointed, and very many of them were remorselessly sold out in consequence; and although their successors have learnt comparative punctuality, still not a year passes without numbers of their estates falling by default into the hands of the Board of Revenue. These, previously to 1871, were almost invariably put up to auction, and with all their license of abuse intact, knocked down to the highest bidders; but during the too brief Lieutenant-Governorship of Sir George Campbell began to dawn what, let us hope, may turn out to be a brighter day. Sir George commenced by ordaining that the sale of forfeited estates should be deferred until all rights of sub-tenants had been fully inquired into and recorded, the old offices of village and district accountant and registrar being re-instituted for the purpose; and he subsequently proceeded to enjoin that the re-settlement should be effected either with the village headmen or with the villagers themselves, the rights of the latter to hold their lands, subject to the payment of fair rents, being in either case recognized and recorded. These are steps so manifestly in the right direction, that perseverance in the same path will probably suffice for the attainment of as much amelioration of the actual order of things as is now practicable, consistently with observance of the engagements into which the Government has heedlessly entered. The deviation from long-established routine is, indeed, as wide as it is salutary. With the Bengal revenue school it has always been a maxim that, in no circumstances whatever, should the Government deal directly with the individual ryots, whereas the more eligible course would seem to be the opposite one of invariably dealing with the ryots, either collectively or individually, wherever the recognized rights of an intermediate class do not interpose a bar. Wherever the continued existence of village communities affords a presumption that such associations are still congenial to actual social conditions, village communities may, for reasons presently to be noted, well deserve to be preferred as the unit for assessment; but that in one way or the other, whenever by good fortune the ryots are restored to their original condition of immediate contact with the State, they should be suffered to remain there, instead of being placed in subjection to newly and needlessly imported middlemen, ought to be as clear as the duty of Government to act, not with favoritism, but with impartiality, and to protect the interests of the many instead of sacrificing them for the aggrandizement of the few.

The practical inference is that, whenever henceforward a Bengal zemindarree falls again by default to the disposal of Government, search should not be made for a new zemindar to replace the old one, and to be invested with the permanent tenure which the latter has forfeited, but that, in whatever measure it be deemed advisable to concede fixity of tenure, the concession should be made to the immediate occupiers of the soil, leases being granted to them for twenty or thirty years, or other adequate periods, at fixed rents representing a certain proportion of the gross produce of the soil. The gain, economic, social, and political, would be immense, even though the concession stopped here; but the additional gain might in all probability repay the additional sacrifice a hundred-fold if the Government should further pledge itself to renew the leases as often as they expired, and to content itself on each renewal with such increase of rent as would preserve the original proportion between the total amount and the gross produce of the soil. The State would in that case retain intact its perpetual right to appropriate at specified intervals a reasonable share of the increment, unearned or other, of the land's value, while the utmost quantity of proprietary right that could, consistently with such reservation on the part of the State, be transferred to individuals, would be transferred to precisely those individuals most likely and best able to utilize it for the general advantage.

Application of the same principle seems to be what is chiefly required in order to bring about such reforms as are still practicable in Oude and in the North-West Provinces. In the former region, some spendthrift 'barons,'[1] as the admirers of the new-fangled Oude aristocracy delight to call them, will no doubt every now and then fall hopelessly into arrear, when an opportunity will present itself for a re-settlement with the peasantry by the grant to them of long and continually renewable leases on conditions similar to those suggested for the ryots of Bengal. The same plan may be adopted in the North-West whenever any, either of the larger zemindars, or of the village proprietors make default—nor might it perhaps be inconsistent with equity, on the termination of the present thirty-years' settlement, to pension off many even of the solvent zemindars, and to make a ryotwar settlement in the North-West the rule instead of the exception. In the Madras territories, the prevailing settlement is already ryotwar, and does not perhaps stand in need of more than two modifications—those two, however, being somewhat momentous. One is the substitution for continually variable rent of a rent unchangeable, except at the close of a series of years, nor alterable even then, except in a ratio exactly corresponding with any alteration that may have taken place in the value of the land; the other, the leaving it optional with the ryots of a village to be assessed separately or collectively—in the latter case, every individual being held responsible for the full amount of the Government dues. That the option, if conceded, would not be suffered to lie dormant, may be inferred from a curious fact cited by Sir G.

[1] Maharajah Sir Man Sing, K.S.I., 'Chief of the Barons of Oude,' is, according to Sir George Campbell, not an Oude man at all, but nephew of a native of Behar, a trooper in one of the East India Company's regiments of cavalry.

Campbell: 'Madras villages have been found which for half a century had submitted to the farce of a Government assessment on each individual, but had year by year lumped the individual assessments together, and redivided the total in their own way among the members of the community.'

In the Punjab the principles advocated have been for many years in force, and no very material change in the mode of applying them seems to be imperatively called for: indeed, what is here intended to be inculcated is the adoption throughout India of land revenue systems analogous to that of the Punjab. Of that system the most characteristic feature is assessment of the village cultivators, not individually, but collectively—an arrangement which necessarily implies exercise by the village community of considerable corporate authority over its members. This, however, to my thinking, is so far from being an objection that I am disposed to regard as a decided desideratum a far nearer approach to rehabilitation of the village communities in their ancient condition than any that has yet taken place. True, there is one early phase of the village community which must be admitted to be economically indefensible. The primitive custom of periodically dividing the cultivated area, not only amongst all the previous occupants, but also amongst any new families that may have branched off from the old stock, is obviously calculated to promote over-population, and, although maintaining social equality, to terminate in equality, not of well-being, but of indigence. In Russia, where the custom is still very generally observed, this tendency has hitherto been obviated by excessive mortality of children consequent on various maternal malpractices, but it may be expected to produce its natural result whenever Russian mothers leave off feeding their babies with sour rye-pap, baptising them by immersion in the depth of winter, and doing certain other things which need not be here particularized. In Java, population is advancing with unparalleled rapidity, doubling in twenty-five years by mere excess of births over deaths, whereas in the United States of America, even with the help of immigration, thirty years are required for similar doubling; and in some parts of the island, the peasants finding their tenements reduced to a third or a fourth of the size of those occupied by their fathers, are petitioning the Government to forbid partition from descending much below an acre.[1] Even in Switzerland, ugly symptoms are beginning to show themselves of the operation of the same cause, which, if left unchecked, may at no distant date go far towards neutralizing the beneficial influence of the *allmends* so highly, and on the whole so justly, eulogized by M. De Laveleye. In India, however, the periodical partition referred to is at present only exceptional, and confined almost entirely to a few of the aboriginal hill tribes. In the plains it has long been a thing of the past, whatever prescriptive rights of occupancy appertain to the ryots being now recognized as permanent rights, and no one being liable to be forcibly dispossessed of part of his patrimony for the endowment of a landless clansman. But, even after having outgrown any unduly populating

[1] Laveleye, *La Propriété*, p. 64, 65.

tendency, and also after ceasing to enjoin routine practices, or otherwise to interfere with the discretion of individual cultivators, the village commune may still seem to be obnoxious to serious reproach. Collective fiscal responsibility, although, as already intimated, to a great extent counterbalanced both by the individual sense of common duty which it naturally engenders, and by the communal power over defaulters necessarily accompanying it, cannot but be pernicious in so far as it constrains the industrious to pay for the idle and dissolute, the thrifty for the improvident; and the tenderness, too, apt to be shown to defaulters, by preventing their displacement by enterprising strangers, may also seem to be obstructive of agricultural progress. But even though these objections were better founded than they are, there would still be social and political considerations more than adequate to outweigh them. The moneyed speculators, by whom so many of the petty landholders of the North-Western Provinces have been bought out, rarely become themselves cultivators, but usually let their newly-acquired properties to a class of tenants, poor enough at first, and rendered subsequently poorer and poorer by the grievous obligations heaped upon them by their usurious landlords. Nor if the reverse were the fact, would it by any means afford matter for unqualified congratulation. Improved husbandry is good, but well-to-do husbandmen are better, and nothing can be worse than the conversion of a large proportion of the ancient husbandmen into outcasts and vagabonds. That rigorous law of contract which we, by long familiarity with it, have come to regard as ethical gospel, but which, as Sir H. Maine has so well shown, is really the tardy product of a somewhat advanced civilization, cannot, without grievous injustice, be strictly enforced against a class of persons whose commercial dealings have been immemorially regulated by custom. About as legitimate would it be for judicial tribunals to act as auxiliaries in holding people to ruinous engagements contracted during their nonage, for in respect to money matters the bulk of Indian ryots are little better than children. They are incapable of comprehending the new-fangled legislation to which they have been subjected by their foreign rulers, or only obtain some glimmer of its meaning on finding themselves hopelessly crushed by it. What they do understand are the institutions and usages of their forefathers; and about the greatest blunder that doctrinaire pedantry has committed, is that of depriving them of the protection which these afforded. What remains is to restore, as far as may be, the old village associations, or at least to annul those fiscal innovations which have led to their decay, and are incompatible with their revival. In the Punjab, fortunately, they are still flourishing, and to resuscitate them pretty generally throughout the Madras and Bombay Presidencies, the North-West and Central Provinces, and partially likewise in Oude and Bengal, might not be difficult, the only indispensable aid thereto on the part of Government being re-settlement of the land revenue when opportunities occur, not with either zemindars or individual ryots, but with the villagers collectively. All the rest might be safely left to the villagers themselves, among whom the instinct of association and traditions of ancestral practice would probably ensure a pretty general institution of councils of elders and the investiture of those councils with such measure of communal authority as might appear most suitable in existing circumstances. This expectation being supposed to be realized, and the leases of the village lands being also assumed to be granted for terms of twenty or thirty years, or other adequately long periods, and to be declared perpetually renewable at rents bearing an invariable proportion to the varying value of the land, let us consider what would be the resulting agrarian organization.

Its basis would be, not precisely a peasant proprietary, but a body of peasant usufructuaries, actuated in a high degree by all the incentives to thrift and industry which peasant proprietorship affords, and surrounded also by conditions of a stability in which a peasant proprietary have too often been found wanting. Every member of the body would be in possession of a holding sufficient for his decent maintenance, which he would not easily be tempted voluntarily to relinquish, of which he would not without extraordinary delinquency be liable to be forcibly deprived, and his tenure of which might moreover be materially strengthened by some further liberality on the part of Government, recommended equally by policy and by equity. Formerly all waste and unoccupied lands were held to belong to the adjoining villages, but under British administration, these, wherever permanent settlements have been made with zemindars, have been made over as a free gift to the latter, and, wherever ryotwar settlements have been effected, have been resumed by the State. In few ways, however, could the State more effectually promote both public and private interests than by restoring some portions of waste to the villages to which they originally appertained, to be held as inalienable and indivisible common property. Such restitution would be tantamount to establishment in India of those *allmends* which, more perhaps than anything else, have contributed to render the lot of the Swiss peasantry among the most enviable of its kind which the world has ever seen. As in the cantons of Uri, Schwytz, Glarus, Appenzell, and Unterwalden, to every privileged commoner, so to every privileged Indian ryot would, by his connexion with the indivisible common domain, be then assured, over and above his private means, pasture for a cow or two, wood for fuel and for building or repairing his dwelling, and a certain quantity of garden produce. Whoever would know how effectually the poorest might by this arrangement be raised above absolute destitution, and how much it may add to the well-being of the better off, should not neglect to read the singularly interesting account given by M. De Laveleye of its operation in Switzerland.

Nothing, however, can be farther from the intention of these pages than to recommend that the State should take any extraordinary pains with the view of bolstering up village communities. The surest proof of accordance of those associations with surrounding social conditions, and of their consequent fitness to endure, would be their ability, when allowed perfectly free internal play, to maintain themselves without external help; if ever they ceased to be in harmony with popular wants and feelings, it would be well that they should perish, and any artificial props that impeded their decay would operate as baneful trammels. No legal restrictions, therefore, should be suffered to prevent them from relaxing the bonds by which they were held together, from conveying to individual freeholders full power to dispose at their discretion of their respective freeholds, or from permitting any number of these from being welded together, by purchase or inheritance, into estates of greater magnitude. Although a quasi-peasant proprietary has been spoken of above as a fitting basis for a future agrarian system, it is by no means contemplated as suitable for superstructure as well as basis. Standing beside and intermingled with the proprietary ryots, there would from the beginning be abundance of zemindars, talookdars, hereditary headmen —private landlords in short of every degree—occupying positions to which any ryot whose ambition pointed that way might aspire, and exhibiting too by their various modes of management the comparative merits of different kinds of landed tenure. If, in the natural course of things, these larger landholders increased continually in number, their multiplication would presumably be a national advantage, nor could the most zealous advocate of peasant proprietorship reasonably regret that his favourite dispensation was giving way to one proved by experiment to be preferable. I have myself no belief that anything of the kind would ever happen; but meantime, at all events, and as long as communal peasant proprietorship survived, it would doubtless be attended by its usual happy effects. Together with extension of the Punjabee agrarian system, there would doubtless be a co-extensive diffusion of the Punjabee agrarian prosperity. Doubtless, under its protection, would everywhere grow up a peasantry as thriving, as contented, and as loyal as that which the region of the Five Rivers is already able to offer in contrast to the rural destitution of many other portions of our Indian empire. Presumably too, the prosperity thus created and fostered would be continually progressive. With every advance in agricultural productiveness, with every rise in the value of agricultural produce, the gains of the actual cultivators would increase—and, what here is specially noteworthy, the beneficial influence of public works would extend largely to the same class. The ryots would participate abundantly in the good done by canals of irrigation in increasing the fertility of the soil, and by railways in facilitating access to market. Their fair share in returns from these investments of public money would no longer be, as at present, almost entirely intercepted by the zemindars.[1]

There is always and everywhere more or less risk that the accomplishment of hopes like those just indulged

[1] 'It has been ruled by the High Courts, both of Calcutta and the North-Western Provinces, that, under the existing law, tenants with rights of occupancy are liable to enhancement of their rents, when the productive powers of their land have been increased by improvements made at the expense either of the landlord *or of the Government.*'—Observations on Indian Finance, by Sir John Strachey, p. 35.

in may be frustrated by that greatest of social evils and foster-mother of all the rest, over-population. As a whole, indeed, India is very far from being over-peopled. A total of 193,000,000 inhabitants, on a total area of 943,600 square miles, gives an average of only 203 to the square mile. In the North-West Provinces, the average is 378; in Oude, 465; in the Punjab, 172; in the Central Provinces, 109; in the Berars, 131. Even in the Bengal Provinces, although the average of Burdwan is 573, of Patna 553, and of Rajeshaye 500, these proportions are not prodigiously in excess of the English average of 422. General averages, however, are very apt to cause us to overlook particulars, and those just cited will be very misleading if they blind us to the fact that, in certain tracts, population is of a density scarcely to be paralleled in any other country. Such, for instance, is the case in a portion of the Damoodah valley, of about 1,000 square miles in extent, bounded by the Rivers Hooghly and Damoodah on the east and west, and by the East Indian Railway and the Oolabariah Canal on the north and south; where, according to Colonel Haig, the rural inhabitants, irrespectively of townspeople, are no fewer than 940 to the square mile, while the average yield of the soil, even in good years, is not more than equivalent to a pound of rice per head per day. For the inevitable misery of which this is but a single example, selected from several of a like character, British administration must be confessed to be in a great degree reponsible, although in a sense implying the reverse of reproach. Under previous domination, Hindoo or Moslem, population had probably been for ages virtually stationary—its stationaryness being, indeed, almost indispensable to the continuance of the Hindoo institution of caste; since scarcely, except on that condition, could children, from generation to generation succeeding to the occupations of their fathers, derive a livelihood from their hereditary callings. They might do this as long as natural causes combined with customs, natural and unnatural, to keep down their numbers; as long as cruel disease and crueller superstitions were suffered without let or hindrance to do their daily deadly work; while war from time to time mowed down myriads, and famine and pestilence with periodical regularity swept away millions. We, however, have changed all this. We have everywhere established internal tranquillity, have suppressed infanticide and suttees, have introduced vaccination, scattered dispensaries and infirmaries broadcast, widely diffused some smattering of medical knowledge, and confronted drought and its train of epidemics with heroic intrepidity. But

> Naturam expellas furcâ, tamen usque recurret.

Nature, when her course is artificially stemmed in one direction, seldom fails to break out with redoubled violence in a fresh place: in order to be kept within bounds she must be invested on all sides. We have neutralized the agencies by which she would have sternly corrected the excesses of her own instincts, and we have before us, in consequence, a mass of misery which her ravages would have prevented, and which threatens to become fifty-fold greater than any which her direst ravages could have occasioned. Is then the humane policy we have adopted simply mistaken kindness? Whether it be so or not is of small practical moment, for of those most disposed so to regard it and to regret its result, there can be none so cold-blooded as to desire that the policy should be reversed. Tremendous as is the problem we have challenged, face it we must—never for one faint-hearted moment shrinking from it as insoluble. Unless ours be a mission of civilization, there is no warrant for our continued presence in India as rulers. As long as we retain that position, we are bound to accept all its responsibilities, on condition, too, of abdicating if we find ourselves unequal to them. And, in truth, our great mistake is almost the reverse of the one suggested; we may have been premature in our application of advanced occidental ideas to backward oriental races, but our error consists less in having done what we have, than in not striving to do more. We have removed the old physical obstacles to over-population without replacing them by moral substitutes, and it is now incumbent on us forthwith to set about repairing the omission. Not improbably, by proceeding to recommend as one means thereto, the communal peasant proprietorship, on whose other merits I have already so much insisted, I shall provoke a compassionate smile from those old-fashioned economists, if any such there still are, in whose eyes the strongest reproach to peasant proprietorship is its supposed tendency to indefinitely stimulate population; but this charge I have elsewhere [1] met with an array of historical and contemporary evidence, which, since my most determined opponents have not ventured to question its validity, I may excusably, perhaps, regard as conclusive. Of all moral impediments to excessive multiplication of the species, there is none so powerful as an elevated standard of material well-being; a sufficient proof of its efficacy is the frequency with which wealthy families everywhere die out for lack of offspring; and we have only to cross the Straits of Dover to discover how close a concomitant it is upon peasant proprietorship. That in India, as elsewhere, peasant proprietorship would exert something of the same prudential influence cannot reasonably be doubted; but in India, unluckily, there are counteracting causes at work which might seriously disturb its natural operation. In that country the procreation of children ranks as highly among religious duties as their baptism does in Europe, and its neglect is held to be punishable with equally awful penalties. Where to die without leaving behind a son to perform one's funeral obsequies is supposed to be almost equivalent to signing a warrant of eternal self-damnation, connubial imprudence is naturally of small account, and all possible precautions are as naturally taken against childlessness; both sons and daughters are at a very early age provided with mates by all orthodox and right-minded parents; the re-marriage of widowers is encouraged; polygamy is sanctified. In such circumstances, mere augmentation of the means of

[1] A Plea for Peasant Proprietors, chap. ii.

livelihood may well fail of its accustomed effect, and may rather act in the opposite direction by enabling a larger proportion of children to be reared to maturity. There can be no trustworthy safeguard against over-population without a modification of the popular religious creed, and this is a change which can scarcely be brought about without the aid of a special agency, to wit, Education, with a few remarks on which subject this volume may appropriately conclude.

CHAPTER VII.

NATIONAL EDUCATION.

OF the many important points connected with this great subject, not more than one or two will here be touched upon. The number of educational institutions in British India, governmentally maintained or aided, is understood to be about 40,000, at which instruction is given to about 1,300,000 pupils, at an expense to the State of between 700,000*l.* and 800,000*l.* What is here proposed to be shown is, first, how little good is done by so much—by far the larger portion—of this outlay as is absorbed by vernacular instruction; and, secondly, how very much more good might be done by applying it to the teaching of English.

There is no great use in a key without some lock which it will fit, nor in being able to construe a language in which there are no books. Now, although in every hundred of Indian National Schools there may, perhaps, be one with an English class, in the remaining ninety-nine vernacular dialects alone are employed; and in no living Indian vernacular are there any books. This assertion will be no sooner heard than contradicted; but even though it be forthwith confronted by an Oordoo Bible, or a Teloogoo or Tamil primer, it need not on that account be withdrawn. If, as Johnson once remarked to his biographical satellite, I complain that there is no fruit in an orchard, what does it matter that some one comes presently, exclaiming, 'Sir, you are mistaken; you said there was no fruit, and see, here are two apples and three pears?' When saying that there are no Indo-vernacular books, of course I mean none to speak of; and certainly of most of such as there are, the less said the better. In the first place, with the exception of some half-dozen classics of the Bagh-o-Bahar type, they are all translations; and in the second, these translations are the work, not of natives, but of foreigners. In quality, as in quantity, the vernacular literature of India is much what that of Wales would be if composed exclusively of works done into Welsh by English philo-Cymrians, who had learnt Welsh for the purpose; or what that of Romanized Britain would have been if it had consisted solely of Cimbric or Celtic translations from the Latin by Roman missionaries. As it happened, the Roman missionaries who crossed over by whole armies to our shores, came with pikes, not books, in their hands: stern, hard-headed propagandists, too, they were, with strong sense, clear views, and no superfluous sentiment. To these it was plain that if the Britons were to learn to read, they had better learn in a language in which there was already plenty of legible material, than in one in which all such material had still to be composed. But they took no pains to teach; they contented themselves with making it the interest of the pupils to learn. Instead of schools, they established law and police courts, custom-houses, and inland revenue and recruiting offices, where all business was transacted in Latin, without some knowledge of which, consequently, no suitor could have the satisfaction of knowing why he was cast in damages or into prison; nor any householder why the tax-gatherer's demand was raised ten per cent., or why his son, and not his neighbour's, was pressed for legionary service. The Romans, besides, were in the habit of planting colonies in all their conquered territories, sometimes putting a detachment of discharged soldiers or civic adventurers in possession of one-third of the houses and lands of an existing city; sometimes assigning to them an adequate area wherein to build a city for themselves. At first these colonists would constitute a patrician order, to whom the rest of the townsfolk stood in the relation of plebeians; but, before long, the privileges of *commercium* and *connubium* would be conveyed to the latter, and the two classes would intertrade and intermarry; whereupon the blood relations of indigenous brides would have an extra motive for acquiring the speech of the high foreign families they had become connected with; and indigenous shopkeepers, even if acquainted with any other written characters, would find it more convenient to keep their accounts in those of their wealthiest customers.

The operation of these various causes was remarkable both for the constant occurrence of certain results, where certain conditions were present, and for the absence of those results wherever the same conditions were absent. Wherever there was a native literature, there also the native language had too firm a hold on the affections of the people to be displaced. Athenians and Corinthians might possibly condescend to pick up a few Latin phrases for occasional dealings with such of their conquerors as did not try to save them the trouble by learning Greek; but they had no idea of deserting Homer for his pale reflection in Virgil, or their original Menander for his travesty in Terence. So they, and Jews likewise, and Syrians and Egyptians, went on reading their own authors, and venting their scorn and spleen against Italian barbarians in their own mother-tongue; and the consequence is, that wherever any living representatives of any of these ancient peoples still abide, their ancient language abides with them. In whatever region the population was at any time chiefly Greek, Greek is still spoken; Coptic still lingers in Egypt; Hebrew in all synagogues, and Syriac in many Eastern churches. Among all the unlettered provincials, on the other hand, a complete linguistic revolution was rapidly effected. The subject barbarians, finding that they could not get on without some acquaintance with their rulers' form of speech, made acquaintance with it accordingly; and, having no patriotic reason for burdening themselves with two sets of words where one would suffice, while taking up a foreign language, let their own drop. Among Gauls and Iberians, Latin became so thoroughly naturalized, that, in spite of its frequent and copious alloy by Franks, Burgundians, and Normans, Goths, Vandals, and Arabs, it still continues the main stock and stay of French and Spanish. In Dacia, even in the brief period allowed for its establishment in that last won and first lost of Roman provinces,

Latin seems to have taken even deeper root, the ordinary discourse of the modern Roumans of Wallachia and Moldavia being made up so largely of Latin words inherited from their Dacian ancestors, that any tolerable Latinist is said to have little difficulty in understanding them. Nor, perhaps, would such an one's facility of intelligence have been less among descendants of the Romanized Britons, if the Angles, Frisians, and Northmen, by whom these were successively conquered, had not, by nearly exterminating them, prevented their leaving any recognizable posterity. That in India the application of like causes would have produced like effects, may be inferred from the completeness with which, in the valley of the Ganges, from Hurdwar as far as Patna, Hindee, under the domination of Persian-speaking Moguls, became supplanted by Oordoo and Hindostanee—mongrels between itself and Persian. Presumably, then, Hindostanee would in turn have been similarly supplanted, if certain parts of the policy of the Moguls had been adopted by their successors. The Anglo-Indian Government, however, has always gone upon a directly opposite tack. Although, for a lengthened period, rigidly excluding natives of India from all offices but the humblest, it from the beginning prescribed the use of the native languages for most administrative details. Instead of furnishing its native subjects with motives for learning its language, it has tried to force its English servants to learn theirs, making a certain proficiency in one or more of the native dialects an indispensable condition of promotion, civil or military. As for any imitation of Roman *municipia*, that was about the last thing to be thought of during the sway of the East India Company, whose constant bugbear was a vision of interlopers, scheming at one time to upset their commercial monopoly, and at another to build up, on the ruins of their territorial domination, an independent confederacy, modelled after that of the United States of America. Within the last thirty years, indeed, the Government has, as we have seen, established a vast number of seminaries of every degree; but in such of these as are intended for the bulk of the people, it has, with unprovoked perversity, instead of encouraging, been at considerable pains to discourage, the study of English. In a celebrated dispatch, addressed by them in 1854, to their Governor-General, the late Court of East Indian Directors lay it down as a principle that the right medium of education is the vernacular languages, the substitution for which of English they earnestly and repeatedly deprecate; and the injunctions thus conveyed have ever since been acted upon with unquestioning fidelity. A special committee, reporting in 1856 on the state of affairs in Bengal, complains of the large proportion of grant-in-aid schools that had originated 'in the growing desire for English education, and were fitted only to meet the wants of those who desired to obtain 'some knowledge of English at a cheap rate, and without the inconvenience of absence from home;' and declare themselves 'unanimously of opinion' that the tendency of such schools is to 'aggravate a very serious evil.'[1] In 1867,

[1] In much the same spirit, even one usually so superior as Colonel Chesney to class or local prejudice, after observing that 'the

an Under-Secretary to the Government of India, remarking that 'to secure to their children a knowledge of our tongue is the one object for which, as a rule, the people are willing to pay,' infers that it is *therefore* necessary to watch lest the desire for the acquisition of English 'have the *evil* tendency' apprehended by the above-quoted committee. In the North-West Provinces, according to the Education Reports for the last few years, there is a rapidly increasing desire for the acquisition of English, 'which, however, is as yet chiefly taught as a language, and not made to supersede the vernacular as a medium of instruction.' In the Punjab, says the local Director-General of Public Instruction in 1863, the neglect of vernacular studies for the purpose of learning English has been 'specially prohibited,' and 'the attention of district and educational officers has been repeatedly directed to the prevention of that *evil.*' 'In a movement,' says the same functionary in 1867, 'for promoting oriental education and vernacular literature, which was started at Lahore two years ago, and has been pressed, under the Lieutenant-Governor's patronage, on the attention of all Government officials and native chiefs and gentlemen, I, to some extent, cordially sympathize,' notwithstanding that it has, as he adds, 'had a bad effect on the progress of English education.' In Oude, says the Director-General of that province, 'in nearly all the Anglo-

tendency of the times is, unquestionably, to obtrude English ways and modes of thought, as well as English speech, into Indian affairs generally,' adds that this is 'not the less from some points of view to be regretted.' Indian Polity, p. 276.

vernacular schools, the boys would, if permitted, give their whole time to their English lessons; and I have been repeatedly asked by pupils and parents to send an English teacher, it being generally added, that compliance with the request would double the attendance.' Nevertheless, in the schools in question, the vernacular alone is still used 'as a medium for imparting knowledge in general subjects, whilst English is read merely as a language.' In the Central Provinces, students of English, for the avowed purpose of diminishing their number, are 'required to pay a higher fee than merely vernacular scholars.' Of the Madras Presidency much the same story is told. A similarly increasing demand for English is observed, and opposed there. Spite of the enlightened efforts of Sir C. Trevelyan and others, to introduce a more judicious system, 'in talook schools, and in the lower classes of zillah schools, English is taught merely as a language, substantive knowledge being conveyed through the medium of the vernacular.' Finally, of the Bombay territories it is emphatically declared, that 'English education has been starved there in the interest of vernacular.' Desire for the former 'manifests itself in constant applications from the people for schoolmasters able to teach English,' for whose maintenance, moreover, 'special subscriptions are offered;' but the people's shepherds continue indisposed to afford them access to the wished-for pasturage. 'At first,' says the Bombay Report for 1865–6, 'there was a tendency in the local committees to seek the extension of English to the neglect of vernacular schools,' but it exultingly adds, 'a resolution of Government has authoritatively settled that point, and now no assignments of local funds to English education are made,' unless the collector of the district can furnish a certificate that its wants 'in respect of vernacular education' have been as far as possible supplied. 'Probably,' says the Report for 1865–6, 'ten per cent. out of the whole number of boys in Government schools are learning English;' but 'the acknowledged tendency to acquire the language of good appointments has been somewhat checked, partly by an order requiring a certain knowledge of his own vernacular before a boy is allowed to begin English; partly by want of sanction for the improvement or establishment of Anglo-vernacular schools, much asked for by the people, and very necessary to this department.'

Three peculiarities in Anglo-Indian administration have now been noted, all of which may, by unprejudiced observers, be not improbably deemed to stand in need of reversal. It would, however, be an abuse of a publicist's privilege of discursiveness to enter at all largely, under the heading of this chapter, either upon the suitableness of India for military colonization, or on the expediency of substituting, in the transaction of revenue and judicial business, the language of the rulers for that of the ruled. On one of these points be it therefore simply suggested, that to attach time-expired men of European regiments to Indian soil, by grants of land on mountain slopes or elevated levels, to be held on condition of occasional military service, might be a very cheap, yet, under proper supervision, a very efficient mode of reinforcing the Anglo-Indian garrison. Whatever might be the technical aptitudes, there could at any rate be no doubt of the loyalty of such a militia, well aware, as it would be, of the sort of disembodiment awaiting it in the event of the *de facto* Government being subverted. With regard to the other, let us figure to ourselves the position of an immigrant Frenchman who, after a year or two's naturalization in Leicester Square, should be commissioned to Zummerzetshire as president of a County Court, or as Sheriff Depute to Aberdeen awa,' and we may then have some faint notion of the difficulties of an Anglo-Indian, ordered as Magistrate, Judge, or Collector, now to Rohilcund, then to the Punjab, and anon recalled to Calcutta ; or moved backwards and forwards between Dharwar and Sind, or between Ganjam and Trichinopoly ; or settled down in that perfect Babel of tongues, the Central Provinces.

The sort of instruction, however, best fitted for adoption in Indian schools, is an affair regularly and immediately before us, and, in connection with it, we may at the outset remark that for purveyors of knowledge, as for those of any other class of wares, the surest plan for attracting customers is to be prepared to supply whatever articles are most in demand. If young Bengal, in search of a hat, enter a shop where only turbans are kept, he may, possibly in despair, fit himself with one of the latter, but quite possibly, too, he may leave without top-gear of any sort. And as with the outer, so with the inner garniture of the head. If he seek for English where only the vernacular is to be acquired, he is as likely as not to try to make shift without either. True, in respect of instruction, those who are most in want are often the least conscious of their want, and oftener still, are the least able to judge what special kind of knowledge it is they need. In India, however, native instinct would seem to have come to a juster conclusion on this last point than English ratiocination. Early Anglo-Indian educationists, indeed, did not aim very high, and did not disproportion ends to means so much as their successors. Even Lieutenant-Governor Thomason—keen-sighted as he was, did not, when propounding his views in 1846, look beyond 'enabling zemindars and cultivators to understand village accounts and the putwari's papers,' for which humble purpose a moderate acquaintance with native pothooks might suffice. But a few years later, more extended views came to be entertained, for we find the East Indian Directors in 1854 dwelling on the shortcomings of Asiatic learning in respect of science, philosophy, and all modern discoveries and improvements, and on the desirableness of supplementing its deficiencies from European stores. But they at the same time evinced great anxiety that Western thought should be communicated principally through Eastern speech. They were content that, in colleges and high schools, European culture should continue to be imparted to the initiated by its own proper sounds and symbols; but they insisted that for popular education the principal instruments should be the vernacular dialects, which, they added, in order to be fitted for the function, should be enriched by translations from the best English elementary treatises. said translations being advertised for and liberally rewarded. These latter suggestions were worthy of Goldsmith's Beau Tibbs, who, having resolved that his daughter should learn Greek, magnanimously resolved also to learn it himself first, in order to be able to teach her: nay, the 'honourable Court' went considerably beyond the Beau, who is not recorded to have contemplated the composition of a new series of Greek classics, whereas they, having decided on having their subjects taught to read in vernaculars whose name was legion, shrank not from the consequent obligation of providing materials for reading in each vernacular. Some books have accordingly been manufactured to order, and no doubt are of many various degrees of merit and its opposite. But without disputing that among the half-dozen for instance, that have been written in, or translated into, Burmese, the Rev. Mr. Hough's geography, albeit 'without maps,' and Mr. Stilson's arithmetic, are as admirable as they have been officially pronounced to be, we may still be certain that, if so, these, and all such as these, cannot but be exceptions to the ordinary rule. Of what quality are the generality of the compilations and versions in question may be pretty confidently inferred from their being, as already intimated, the performances, not of natives, but of aliens; of the most accomplished of whom it can be no disparagement to say that they are, at any rate, in their several linguistic walks, not more than the equals of Max Müller. Yet, if that prince of living philologists were to attempt lengthened composition in that one, of the many foreign languages he understands, which he more especially and formally professes, the chances are great that he would commit not a few innovations in phraseology as puzzling to pundits as the darkest archaisms of the Vedic hymns. And even if all Indianized specimens of English literature were of unimpeachable quality, their numercial paucity would still be a serious drawback from their educational utility. Doubtless, however scanty were the literature of a language, it might possibly be worth learning that language for the sake of its literature. Few as are the publications that have been provided for the edification of the blind, any one, disqualified for seeing his way through those few, might do well to learn to feel it. But it would be a sad waste of labour for those to learn to read by touch who, by being taught to read by sight, could acquire equal command over books prepared for either purpose, either for manipulation or inspection. Nor would those pains be much more wisely directed which were spent in gaining access to a small fraction of any particular literature in translation, when, without much more trouble, the whole of the same literature might be rendered equally accessible in the original. Of course the applicability of this remark depends upon the relative degrees of trouble required for the two operations; but although it is no doubt easier to learn to read in one's own than in a foreign language, the difference of difficulty is much less than is commonly supposed. Time was when throughout Western Europe, whatever child was taught his A B C, was taught it out of a Latin primer, and presently afterwards had to get his grammar likewise by heart in Latin, as Eton youngsters had, till almost the other day, without the faintest glimmer at first of the sense of what he was required to repeat. Here truly was pursuit of knowledge under difficulties, which yet was rapidly and eminently successful. Of the 5,000 students who, towards the close of the eleventh century gathered round Abelard at Paris, or of the 30,000 with whom contemporaneous Oxford has been peopled by the prolific imagination of Anthony à Wood, a large proportion were literally mendicants, as absolutely dependent, as the autobiography of Thomas Platter owns him to have been, on the broken victuals they got by begging. These, having come of parents too poor to furnish them at all abundantly with educational means and appliances, had commonly learnt their rudiments at a hedge-school, presided over by the parish curate, or by a monk from a neighbouring convent. Yet without better preliminary training than was thus obtainable, numbers of youths were continually reaching the universities, fully prepared to listen with keen zest to the erudite doctors they found disputing there, and to take notes of their Latin discourses. It is not, in short, too much to affirm that, during the earlier part of the Middle Ages, almost every one who had been to school was as well able to read and write in a dead foreign language as he would have been in his own living mother-tongue, if the latter instead of the former had been employed for his scholastic tuition. A parallel and more recent case is afforded by educational experience in the northernmost half of North Britain. When Walter Scott, some eighty years ago, was taking in the Highlands those sketches from life which he subsequently worked up into finished pictures under the names of 'Waverley' and 'Rob Roy,' few of the aborigines, below the degree of Duinhé Wassel, were qualified to hold oral converse with the Southron. Two or three intervening generations, however, have given quite another turn to the linguistic difficulty. Where there used to be so few who could speak English, the number is now fast diminishing of those who can speak much else, insomuch that patrons of Highland livings, notwithstanding the number of sons of small farmers and small shopkeepers bred up in Scotland to the church, are occasionally at a loss for ministers qualified for induction into their vacant benefices by that acquaintance with Gaelic which ecclesiastical ordinances prescribe. In all the primary schools, of which—thanks principally to the General Assembly—there is now a tolerable sprinkling over the whole stretch of country between the Ochil Hills and the Pentland Firth, all pupils are taught English; at which many of them, before finally leaving, become little less apt than the generality of English-born boys of similar age and social standing, the English of the former being, indeed, much more of the grammar and dictionary species than that of the latter—more correct that is, and freer from colloquial vulgarisms. That these young Gaels, priding themselves on their new accomplishment, and valuing it for its extensive utility, should sport it on most occasions to the proportionate neglect of its native rival, is easily understood. Neither is there anything surprising in their acquiring it so readily. As long as initiation into the mysteries of scholastic learning is required to consist of committal to memory of a number of unmeaning sounds, it will not greatly matter what those sounds are, whether English or Latin, Gaelic or English, or yet Indo-vernacular or English. Neither, as long as the memory remains unincumbered, is much more exertion requisite for taking in two sets than one set of words, as may be seen from the facility with which, wherever four or five languages are commonly spoken, children imbibe them all—in many Levantine cities, for instance, talking Greek, Turkish, French, and Italian with equal fluency.

It need not be doubted then, that the counterpart of what takes place in the Scottish Highlands, might by corresponding arrangements, be equally brought about in India. By the adoption of suitable means, an English bent may as readily be given to the young idea of Gentoo as of Gael, and it is satisfactory to note what simple means may apparently suffice for the purpose. What the ruling powers have to do in the matter is not so much to encourage as to leave off discouraging; not so much to stimulate the already great and rapidly-growing desire for specific instruction, as to cease from withholding the desired instruction from those who seek it. The alteration most needed in the present educational system is, that in all Government seminaries of every degree, in the lowest as well as in the highest, adequate provision should be made for teaching English. This being done, it might perhaps be safely left optional with parents whether their children should learn English, and whether, if they did, they should have lessons in the vernacular likewise; for, to judge from evidence already referred to, there can be little doubt what the usual decision would be. No doubt it is not in Oude only that the pupils, 'if permitted, would give their whole time to their English lessons.' Still, if only for the sake of adherence to some intelligible principle, it might be better that English should be made an obligatory subject in all schools, as it is already in all colleges, the study of any vernacular being at the same time left optional, or even excluded, except as an auxiliary to the study of English. Among Anglo-Indian educationists a much vexed question is, whether the national mind can be most speedily and thoroughly permeated by filtration from above or capillary attraction from below, but without venturing to decide between the two plans, we may reasonably assume that a judicious mixture of both would be better than either. If, while the three Presidency Universities and their affiliated colleges were sending annually increasing numbers of native young gentlemen to shine forth as literary and scientific lights, and kindle emulative flames among their social inferiors, middle-class pupils were being prepared at zillah, tehsil, and circuit schools for entrance on a college course, and lower and lowest class pupils were being similarly prepared at primary schools for middle-class instruction, it may reasonably be supposed that the educational currents thus proceeding from opposite extremities of the social scale would meet half-way in about half the time that would be required for either to traverse the whole intervening distance. Some cause has already been shown for supposing that the two converging currents would require but little more time to meet on account of their having become streams of English knowledge, and in addition to other reasons for thinking that the whole time required would not be great, the following may be stated. In certain districts of Lower Bengal the bulk of the native reading public are even now so far Anglicized as, not only to have their book-shelves filled with English volumes, but to prefer that the 'Hindoo Patriot' and other like newspapers, expressly designed to be vehicles and reflectors of native thought, should be composed in English. Now as, of the educational influences which have directly contributed to this result, few have been in active operation for much more than a generation, it would seem that, with better management and directer application of means to ends, the same result might be produced elsewhere within a very moderate multiple of the same period. Many improvements in educational practice might have to be made, and some educational expedients, which as yet exist only in theory, might have to be adopted in order to ensure success; but if the authority on which success would mainly depend, took up the work in earnest, there is nothing very extravagant in imagining that, in two or three generations hence, English might become naturalized all over India in the same degree as it already is in parts of Bengal proper. And, of course, a linguistic revolution which had proceeded so far would not stop there, but would go on advancing with continually accelerated steps, until of difference of speech, that fruitful source of graver differences, few traces should remain between Britain and her magnificent dependency.

In the prospect of the eventual supersession of all Indo-vernaculars which the supposed diffusion of English implies, there is, indeed, genuine cause for ethnological regret, in which the present writer would be sorry to be supposed not to participate. Alas! that a single one of the inter-jangling tongues, whose hubbub stopped the building of the tower on Shinar's plain, should be completely hushed, leaving no echo behind. Alas! that there are no longer means of ascertaining whether the pigmy breed of the neolithic period talked as much like the Esquimaux of to-day as they resembled them in their habits, and in the fashion and ornamentation of their implements. Alas! that we may never hope to discover by what shibboleth Pelasgians were distinguishable from Tyrrhenians and Sikelians, or these again from Umbrians, Sabines, or Samnites! Would that the old woman, famous for having been the last to speak Cornish, could have lived for ever! Would that the United States' Government would found professorships of Sioux and Cherokee before the last representatives of the so-named tribes are irrevocably improved off the face of the earth! Almost is it to be wished that civilization may never have such complete possession of India, but that there may still remain some few barbarian hillmen, faithfully adhering to the barbarous dialects of their forefathers. But if this may not be, and if comparative glossologists of a remote future, in default of living embodiments, must content themselves with fossil remains, of the aboriginal tongues, and make the most of such Hindee and Tamil spelling-books as may still be extant, there will yet be abundant compensation for the ethnological loss in the miscellaneous gain, from which it will be the only drawback. For to enumerate only a few, and to begin with one of the least of the many benefits by which India will be rewarded for consenting to exchange her score of illiterate, for a single literate, language, how will not her whole technical industry be stimulated and promoted, when, to every industrial worker, from the ploughman to the experimental chemist, and from the blacksmith to the civil engineer, all the recorded results of England's technical experience are thrown open? How again, when the accumulated fruits of English adventure, in every field of science and literature, are made equally accessible—not simply to some few hundreds of university graduates, but to every one who has made decent use of his time at school—how will not the national intellect be stirred and sharpened? how will not the moral sense be exalted and purified? With all our insular narrow-mindedness, with all our defects in taste and temperament, sensibility and sentiment, with all our snobbishness and Philistinism, our English standards, ethic and æsthetic, our general tone of thought and feeling, are still undeniably far above those of our Eastern fellow-subjects. For the average East Indian to rise to the mental level of the average Briton would surely be an immense ascent—an immense upraising of his ideas of truth, honour, faith, and charity; and among possible aids to such self-elevation, none is more efficacious than literature. As an individual author, in so far as his subject permits, commonly sets forth in his publications the best side of his character, sketching an ideal which he would fain realize if he could, and if indolence or infirmity of purpose did not hinder, so what the literature of every advanced people most prominently reflects are the nation's noblest characteristics; of which native readers, becoming, Narcissus-like, enamoured, strive to become more and more personally possessed, while foreign readers are all the more apt to admire them on account of their comparative novelty. The less, too, of native literature a people possess, the greater is the benefit they are likely to derive from an adopted literature. An intelligent Hindoo, led away from the sapless leaves of his Shasters, and turned loose into the wholesomer pasturage of good English reading, could not help, by assimilation of the fresh provender he browsed upon, being partially renewed in the inner man, and getting some of his old moral tissues replaced by others of a sounder and healthier fibre. Nor would the transmutation thus commenced be readily arrested. If religion be the firmest basis of morality, morality, on the other hand, is seldom improved without reacting powerfully on religion. Perseverance for a few decades in the Anglicizing process above suggested, would do more for Christianity in India than centuries of missionary enterprise. In readiness to compass sea and land to make one proselyte, the agents of modern societies for the propagation of the Gospel in foreign parts may well bear comparison with the Scribes and Pharisees of old; yet how many proselytes have they made? According to the most hyperbolical accounts, the number in an East Indian population of little less than two hundred millions, is little more than as many thousands. It may be a humiliating reflection, but it is at the same time a not disheartening truth, that religious conversion on a large scale is an affair much rather of example than of precept. For the most part, 'e'en as the bell-wether moves on, the docile flock moves too.' When a certain Gothic king, as Gibbon tells us, went up to be baptized, all his Goths went with him; but when he, with one foot in the font, stepped back, because the officiating priests insisted that all his unbaptized ancestors were everlastingly damned, all the Goths stepped back too, sovereign and subjects harmoniously relapsing into idolatry. So in later times, which European states should become Protestant, and which remain Catholic, depended mainly on which monarchs accepted, and which rejected, the teachings of Luther. Again, the marked missionary success of Moravian brethren among the Hottentots and other wild tribes, is mainly due to their having, like the Jesuit fathers in Paraguay and California, endeavoured to civilize before attempting to Christianize, and to establish a secular, before aiming at a religious, influence. Their plan is to gather round them a little community of savages, whom they first persuade to dig and plant, and to build houses, and wear pantaloons and petticoats, and who, beginning thus by imitation of the domestic customs of their teachers, are led insensibly to similar adoption of their religious observances. Presumably, a not less effective mode of Christianizing India might be to begin by Anglicizing its language. This at any rate would be an excellent preparation for the task. Although no course of reading however special, could be depended upon for converting East Indians to any particular creed, there is no course of English reading, however general, that would permit them to retain their present creeds. All the evidences of Paley, and of all his collaborators, might fail to make them Christians; but London newspapers alone would prevent their remaining Pagans or Mohammedans. For anyone to look regularly through the Times, or Daily News, or Spectator, or Saturday Review, not to speak of Monthlies or Quarterlies, or of *the* Fortnightly, and to retain his respect for the Shasters or the Koran, is not in the nature of things. The rude shocks which the Asiatic intellect would receive from many of the veriest commonplaces of English journalism, would rub off much of its traditional rust, and render it freer for the reception of whatever of genuine truth, religious or other, came in its way. And more and more of truth of all sorts would, in the circumstances supposed, be continually coming. In proportion as East Indians became internally Anglicized, and as inward change told upon outward demeanour, they would acquire at once more taste and desire for British companionship, and more congeniality for it. Mutually repelling prejudices, passing away with the occasions for them, would leave immigrant and indigenous races free to coalesce; the former to become Anglo-Indian in a more enlarged and liberal sense; the latter, to assume with equal right the correlative designation of Indo-Britons. Educated members of both would then, without scruple, mix together on equal terms, dining and dancing at each other's houses, walking, riding, picnicking together, and discoursing between whiles; frequenting, too, the same places of public resort, churches and chapels not excepted, which Orientals, we may fairly presume, would be occasionally tempted to visit by the same curiosity, if by nothing better, which attracts Occidentals to mosques and pagodas, and in which some who had come to pry, might possibly now and then remain to pray. Changes of this kind, together with their whole train of easily-conjectured consequences, although commencing in the higher strata of society, would in ordinary course filtrate downwards until the lowermost layer was reached. The leaven cast in at the top would not cease working till the whole lump, from zemindar and baboo to ryot and coolie, was thoroughly leavened. Nor would the process be necessarily a very long one, provided only that evangelizing zeal did not, out of superfervid regard for truth, put up error's back by unseasonably anathematizing error. Provided only that the children of light would consent to practise in their generation somewhat of the wisdom of the children of darkness, but very few generations might perhaps be needed to exalt India to the same religious level as that of Britain—to a level at which the bulk of the population might be described as, in one fashion or another, Christian—part really so and from conviction; a larger part not less sincerely, though chiefly from habit; and a still larger residue in name only and in appearance. Whoever may be disposed to say that a metamorphosis, to be made up so largely of superficial varnish, is not much to look forward to, will do well to ask himself within what time a fiftieth part of the same result could be brought about by other means.

The picture we have been contemplating has yet another aspect—to wit, the political, which there may be more reason for declining to regard with unmingled satisfaction. Could India, it may fairly be asked, be imbued with the English spirit in so many other respects, without imbibing also too much of the English love of independence to continue to acquiesce in English domination? To this inquiry it might be sufficient to reply, that the one sole way in which England can justify her retention of India is by availing herself of it for the benefit of the people, and doing more for them than they are capable of doing for themselves. But of the obligation thus incumbent on her, she can acquit herself only in proportion as she renders India worthy of independence, and she will not have acquitted herself of it completely unless, whenever India shows herself both worthy and desirous of political freedom, she consents to set India free. There are, however, perfectly legitimate means—means which she not only may, but is in duty bound to, employ—of preventing India from desiring independence, even when at length deserving it. As yet, desire in that particular has considerably outrun desert. Although governed, so far as material interests are concerned, not only infinitely better than she ever was before, but with a parental solicitude such as no conquered territory ever before experienced from a foreign stepfather, she is so little satisfied with her British King Log as to be apparently not altogether unwilling to try the experiment of a Russian King Stork in his stead. Nor have we far to seek for an explanation of this anomoly. We have only to ask how we ourselves should like it, if, the British Islands happening to become outlying appendages of the new Prussian Empire, no native-born Briton were suffered to hold a commission in the army, or to rise above a second-class clerkship in the civil service, or above a county court judgeship in the law. Would any or all of the real and substantial advantages that might possibly accompany Prussian annexation—would completest reform of railway mismanagement, or fullest security against garotting, or widest diffusion of intellectual and æsthetic culture, be accepted as compensation for such blockage of all those careers which ordinary ambition most affects? Would not baffled longings turn rapidly into bitter animosity, engendered first among those ardent spirits by whom opinion is formed and directed, and gradually accepted by the docile multitudes who think and feel on all public matters as popular leaders bid them? We have only to consider how our nobility and gentry and moneyed magnates, our professional and literary men, our newspaper writers and stump orators, would, in the circumstances supposed, feel, and show their feelings, towards the powers that were, to understand the feelings of corresponding classes in India towards the powers that actually are. If British rule in India is to be permanent, it must become popular with the natives, which it plainly cannot be while continuing to seethe them, as it were, in their mother's milk, shutting them off from advancement in their own land, avowedly because they were born and bred there. We need not hope to reconcile the children of the soil to the presence amongst them of us strangers, unless we admit them to equality of privileges, and afford them equal facilities of access to, and equal chances of success in, every honourable career; unless every branch of the public service, covenanted or uncovenanted, be freely thrown open to them, and native birth and parentage cease to be disqualifications for any local dignity whatever, even for that of Governor-General or of Commander-in-Chief. To the inevitable outcry against the mere mention of constitutional changes so radical as these, the only reply which space here permits is a slight allusion to analogous experience. When Alexander the Great had conquered Persia, he continued most of Darius's satraps in their stations, and filled up vacant satrapies quite as frequently with Persians as with Europeans. He persuaded, or rather forced, many of his Macedonian captains to marry Persian wives, and not only placed his large levies of Asiatic troops under the command of Asiatic chiliarchs and pentakosiarchs, but officered in part with Persians even his Companion Cavalry, the crack corps *par excellence* of the army which had accompanied him from Europe. The Macedonians murmured, remonstrated, mutinied, but Alexander was obstinate; and the example thus set by him was followed by the Seleucid kings who succeeded by usurpation to the greater part of his Asiatic conquests. Though all the business of their Government was transacted in the Greek language, the functionaries by whom it was transacted must necessarily have been in far larger proportion Hellenized Asiatics than Asiatized Hellenes. It was thus on the support much more of the former than of the latter that the dynasty rested; yet intrusive and Greek as the dynasty was, it lasted for nearly three centuries, and its subversion at last was effected not by domestic insurrection, but by foreign invasion: for, having been wise enough to make no distinction between the conquering and conquered races, it had been served as cheerfully by the one as by the other, the loyalty of the Asiatic portion of the population being probably as little affected by the European origin of their sovereign, as that of Englishmen is by the fact that Queen Victoria's great-great-grandparents were almost pure Germans.

With little other alteration than that of the proper names, this notice of the Seleucidæ of Syria and Babylonia may serve equally for the Mogul and other Mahommedan dynasties of Hindostan, which similarly succeeded in completely conciliating their Hindoo subjects by the simple expedient of employing them, equally with Moslems, in every administrative grade, and whose sway was never threatened by any analogue of the Sepoy mutiny, and, but for English intermeddling, might not impossibly be still subsisting. Christian England ought not to require to learn from heathen Greeks and Mahommedan Moguls that the wisest policy for the government of dependencies is that of doing unto others as we would ourselves be done by; but if willing at length to be so instructed, and to act honestly and consistently on the lesson, she may quite possibly dissipate all that internal discontent which alone can prevent Queens and Kings of England, as long as any such there be, from continuing to be likewise Empresses and Emperors of Hindostan.

Neither, if fate otherwise decree, and if by spontaneous movement, originating in an impulse communicated by England herself, the most lustrous of oriental jewels be severed from the British crown, will this be any detraction from—nay, rather will it be a brilliant addition to, our country's glory. As to every individual, so to every nation, its appointed task in life; its own proper share in the great work of promoting God's kingdom on earth; and to none has been vouchsafed so grand a share as to ourselves. 'England,' said the Prince Consort in a letter to Lord John Russell replete with political wisdom and with elevated and elevating sentiment, 'England, by her own energies, and by the fortunate circumstances in which she has been placed, has acquired a start in civilization, liberty, and prosperity over all other countries. Her popular institutions are most developed and perfected, and she has run through a development which other countries will yet in succession have to pass through. England's mission, duty, and interest, is to put herself at the head of the diffusion of civilization and the attainment of liberty. Let her mode of acting, then, be that of fostering and protecting every effort made by a State in that direction.' So spake one peculiarly interested in the future destinies of our Royal House, nor can worthier counsel be offered to any British or Anglo-Indian statesman. By the latter in especial it deserves to be constantly borne in mind, even as though, to him more particularly, accompanied by the injunction—not the less apposite because lame in one of its feet—

Hæ tibi erunt artes, Britanne, memento!